DOCUMENT FRAUD
AND OTHER CRIMES
OF DECEPTION

DOCUMENT FRAUD
AND OTHER CRIMES
OF DECEPTION

by Jesse M.Greenwald

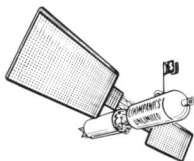

Loompanics Unlimited
Port Townsend, Washington

This book is sold for informational purposes only. Neither the author nor the publisher will be held accountable for the use or misuse of the information contained in this book.

Document Fraud And Other Crimes Of Deception
© 1997 by Jesse M. Greewald

Published by:
Loompanics Unlimited
PO Box 1197
Port Townsend, WA 98368
Loompanics Unlimited is a division of Loompanics Enterprises, Inc.
1-360-385-2230

Illustrations by Holly K. Tuttle
Photos by Donald B. Parker

ISBN 1-55950-155-3
Library of Congress Card Catalog 97-71899

Contents

"The boundaries of a man's imagination are marked by the graves of his dreams."
— Jesse M. Greenwald

"Do your job right."
— *Anonymous convict*

Jesse M. Greenwald
ADC #111856

"Anyone can be conned. It's just that a sucker
will bet you money that he can't be."

Introduction

By the time you have finished reading this book, you will be as informed on the subject of creating and passing false documents as anyone in the business. I have spent the better part of the last twenty-three years making a very good living in the rubber-document field, and thanks to modern technology and its availability, succeeding in this business has never been easier. I will explain what equipment is needed and how and where the forger obtains it, along with support information to assist in understanding its usage. When one has finished reading this book, it should be understandable how, with astonishingly little effort, it is possible to duplicate and pass almost any document commonly used in the business world today.

I will also be explaining the ultimate credit-card scam. That fraud will cover the industry's latest attempt at foiling credit-card fraud: the card with a photo. I will explain how the forger makes almost any of the cards used today, and how he imposes a fraudulent picture on other people's cards. These cards are not stolen; they are just copies of the originals, and are valid for all of the same things that the originals are. I will also explain how this same method is used to obtain legally issued identity cards and driver's licenses.

These processes and some of the others I will discuss are sophisticated and professional. They need to be considered with that in mind. They require an investment of time and money, along with the intelligence to make them work. Most of these scams are not for the beginner, and they require a degree of confidence in ability that only comes from exposure to this type of activity. There are few, if any, experienced fraud criminals whose activities and methods mirror mine. Most people who are familiar with this kind of work have their own way of doing things, and my methods should be viewed as a supplement to that knowledge. Since I have no control over the knowledge or the methods others may possess and use, I will merely explain the tools and their operation. The reader can fill in the blanks.

Once one has mastered the skills of using the equipment, and understands the processes by which the documents are created, those processes can be applied to many variations. It is not complicated or difficult, and aside from the initial setup, it's not really expensive to do. The methods for duplicating most documents are virtually identical, no matter which type of fraud is being perpetrated. Once one has the equipment set up and running, the only limitations will be those imposed by lack of imagination and creativity.

I will discuss each process in enough detail to provide an understanding of the fundamentals. There are always variations, so if I expound on something that seems better suited to someone else's skills or preferred methods, then I recommend following whatever path of study provides the necessary expertise and confidence, in order to obtain a fuller understanding. My way is just one of many, and that is where the reader's brain comes in. After all, the one committing the crime is the person who will benefit or suffer accordingly, and our study of the forger's activities will bear out this dictum.

The modern forger must acquire computer skills. It is not necessary that the forger be a whiz or anything, but a basic understanding and the ability to operate a personal computer with "Windows" and various other office programs are required in order to adequately carry out these undertakings. There are also a rather sophisticated scanner and printer which are used in these processes, but there is nothing that one cannot become proficient in with a couple of days of practice. 20th-century criminals have become adept on computers. The computer and related technologies are the tools of today, not tomorrow, and the laws of the jungle are very simple: adapt or perish.

Chapter One

The Equipment

The obvious first step to creating documents with a computer is to have a computer. If the forger already has a computer, then he need only upgrade it with the needed components and software. If he does not have a computer, then he should get the latest model obtainable. A 386 microprocessor, or better, is sufficient. For most users, the *IBM* system is preferable to an *Apple*. They will both work, but I find that the IBM system is easier for the less-experienced, and the scanner software is easier to use and install. Given the large size of the computer files that the forger will be working with, more RAM (Random Access Memory) is required than the average user usually needs. A very good printer is also desirable, because it is unlikely that the one on hand will do the job. Few people have professional-level equipment in their home.

The first thing we will discuss is the printer. There are lots of printers floating around out there, but few that will actually do the job that needs to be done. If one has a choice, then the *Hewlett-Packard LaserJet III* printer is recommended. They are no longer sold new, but may be found used. The major requirement for the chosen printer is that it must be able to use a magnetic ink character recognition cartridge. This cartridge is called an *MICR,* and its use allows the forger to print items that need to be read with a *"reader."* This device can only read characters that are printed with magnetic ink. Most printers do not have this capability, and the ones that do are not cheap. New printers are being introduced all of the time, so if one is shopping around, this function is a must. The good news is that there are millions of these office-quality printers out there, and finding a used one is not that hard; it should not cost more than $650, but a new one can run up to $2,000. If the shopping forger is asked by a salesperson why this application is needed on his printer, he need only reply that it will be used for on-demand payroll-check printing. That is the most common use for them, and mentioning it will also allow the forger to ask for an MICR, or a place to get one. The HP LaserJet III is a *laser jet* printer, one of the finest document-quality printers on the market, and, in all probability, the only model one will ever need to buy. It does not print in color, but color is not required for the most part. Color needs and applications will be explained in another chapter, along with the best method of achieving them. Ninety-nine percent of the work the forger will have the printer do will be in accordance with the instructions that come with the computer, so there is little more that needs to be said about the printer. It is the actual instrument that documents will be made with, so one should not pinch pennies here.

The next piece of hardware needed is the *scanner*. Hewlett-Packard also makes one of the best models of these devices on the market. The *HP ScanJet 4c* is the scanner of choice, and will do everything required. In computer terminology, it is a *high-resolution, optical character recognition, black-and-white or color, document quality* scanner, with a variable *DPI* (dots per inch) of over 1200. If any of the preceding words sounded foreign, then it should be obvious that additional education in this area is needed. I am not trying to describe a get-rich-quick-overnight scam. If the forger understands what is being explained here, and has the desire to pursue it further, then it should be clearly specified that this is a process which is being described here, not a specific application. It is like any type of sport: once one has the knowledge of it, he still has to enter and participate in the event he chooses. Once the forger acquires and masters these skills, he still has to plan and commit the various offenses which will result in the desired outcome (i.e., the desired income). Knowing how to do it properly only increases the forger's chance of success; it does not automatically make events work out the way he would hope. The scanner (like the printer) is also completely controlled by the computer, so, aside from scanning things on it, all of the instructions go through the PC. This scanner may cost between $500 and $1,000, depending on the upgrades found on it. The forger's needs are simple, and the basic model will work fine, but if the upgrades are offered, they should be taken for later use.

In a nutshell, the scanner is used to copy the documents that the forger intends to duplicate or alter. It takes the images from the items which are put into it, and translates them into information that the computer can understand. Once this information is in the computer, it can then be manipulated into any form desired. If the correct paper is used, the finished product will be an exact duplicate of the original, and will serve the same purpose in its business application. The details that make a document authentic are usually the format and the signature on it. Once one learns how to manipulate these two key elements, almost any document in circulation today can be forged. The scanner will allow the forger to copy and reprint these elements, as well as the safeguards that appear on almost all of the paperwork he will be working with. There are details in most of these documents that will escape the naked eye unless one knows what one is looking for and where they are located. The scanner doesn't care what it sees, it just copies everything and translates it into the computer's memory. When the documents are scanned and reprinted, these safeguards are carried along. The higher the DPI on the scanner, the higher the resolution of the scan and reprint. In English, that means the better the scanner will read the document's details. This is the reason the scanner needs to be of high quality, or "high resolution," as the industry likes to refer to it. All of the components of the system need to be of equal quality and proficiency, or the forger will be frustrated. The correct tools always make the job easier. Don't shop at Kmart and expect Saks' quality.

Chapter Two

The Paper

The next component is the paper required to do the job. Since each job has different paper needs, the best solution to this problem is to get catalogs of the various kinds of papers available in the printing industry. The forger's needs are no different than legitimate needs, so his method of acquisition shouldn't be any different either. The forger has the right to purchase the needed paper just like everyone else does; it's the information about how and where to find such paper that usually keeps the common person from doing this. These catalogs are offered by all of the businesses that sell or distribute paper to the printing industry, and getting one requires only a phone call or a personal visit to the proper company. The phone book might supply some of the names the forger will need, but it is a simple matter to use one of the two major players in the game. They both have offices all over the country and will do business by phone and mail, both methods which I make use of in most business dealings concerning these endeavors. If the forger calls *Rocky Mountain Bank Notes* or *Deluxe Checks, Inc.*, he can obtain a catalog of all of the paper used in the *world* today.

The forger usually gets a mail box under a business name (at a privately run mail drop and not the Post Office), and uses it for all of his business correspondence and transactions. If the forger has a box

6

with 24-hour access, he can come and go at night, and, except for the time when he initially rents the box, avoid the people who work there. Once the forger has rented the box, he need merely call and order the latest catalogs of check and document products that the companies offer. This is their business, and inquiries will be welcome. When connected to a salesman, the forger says that he is getting into the desktop publishing business, and would like to see their catalog for possible purchases. The salesman is told that the prospective buyer will be engaged in on-demand payroll-check printing, and may have other office needs. This is a common desire for the small businessman, and the salesman might include some sample products as an incentive to do business with his company. Encourage this action on the part of the salesman, and the samples will most likely be sent. If the forger asks for samples of their products, he will probably receive a shitload of stuff that could be used later for practice. One loses nothing by asking, and it is remarkable how accommodating the paper suppliers are. These guys offer a wealth of information, and they can answer some of the questions the forger might have that are not covered elsewhere in this book.

The forger should not order anything but the catalog at this time. The objective is to get one's business name entered into the computer files of the company from which materials will be purchased at a later date. Once the catalog has been reviewed, the forger can call back and order what is wanted, as the fraudulent business's name is already listed as a customer in the paper supplier's database. When the forger calls and orders paper, he need merely ask for the order desk and place an order, as if it were an everyday business occurrence. The paper company will probably require some type of prepayment, since they are dealing with a new customer, but COD is also common. The forger must make sure to make arrangements for the COD to be dropped off at his mail box service. A common money order is required, since a company check would require a business account that does not exist and is difficult to establish. It is very unlikely that these activities will ever be traced back to the mail box service, but comings and goings should be kept to a minimum. The forger can place the money order in his box at night, then call the owner of the mail box service the next morning and explain what should be done with it. The mail box service proprietors are usually very easy to do business with in this manner, and normally don't mind helping out a boxholder. The forger might want to order all of the supplies that he thinks will be needed through the mail, and then walk away from the mail box service once they have been obtained and never look back. If the key is left in the box upon departure along with a short note, the note will then be read and thrown into the trash to be forgotten. Businesses come and go all of the time. A fraudulent one will look normal and mean nothing if the shit ever hits the fan. The forger will still have the catalogs and the ability to get more paper when needed. The knowledge is filed away for future reference, and the forger moves on.

The above-mentioned places supply the paper used in printing checks, money orders, stocks and bonds, car titles, birth certificates, diplomas, certificates of deposit, and just about all of the other documents used in the business world today. The forger need only acquire the equipment which is necessary to do the job, and technically he is in the same business as any printing company. Where do you think the bank gets the checks printed that customers order through them? They just call their printer and order some checks with the pertinent information on them. It's no big secret organization or anything, it's just business as usual to a busy printer. If it's not done correctly or at the best price, the bank just shops elsewhere as any other customer would.

The safeguards in this industry are few and easily defeated, and this makes me unhappy, as I do wish it were harder so that more people could be kept out of defrauding it. The phone book is full of companies that provide printing as their business, and they shop daily at many places that supply the paper they require. The forger needs to relax, buy what he needs, and move on. If he cannot achieve this goal, his future in the document-fraud business is doubtful at best.

Chapter Three

The Software

Consider the brain to be a computer. The information and instructions one puts into it are like software. Without instructions and guidelines, the computer would just sit there and beep. Software is how we introduce instructions into the computer, and everything we do on the computer after that introduction is controlled by the programs in that software. Once information is scanned into the computer, changing or manipulating that information requires software which contains a "cut-and-paste" application. This can best be achieved through the "Windows" operating system, which can make such tasks simple to do if there is a version of "Windows" controlling everything. The forger does not need the "Windows 95" version (or anything that expensive), but if he has it, that is fine. When shopping for the software to set this up, the forger tells the salesman his needs, and the salesman will demonstrate several that will do the job. The brand is not important, as long as it has the ability to create new documents and work with a scanner. The good stuff has easy-to-follow instructions. There is no way for me to be more specific than this, as there are thousands of ways to run this setup and its programs. It is helpful to get a version of accounting software such as "Quicken," which is a payroll and checkbook program. Such programs are needed to generate phony checks or create dummy income statements for loan applications. These are just a couple of the software programs one will use. Others will not be needed until more elaborate scams are undertaken. The forger obtains just what is needed in order to get started, and upgrades later. "CorelDraw" is also a very good program for creating and altering documents, and there are several versions available. The forger should try to buy one that is on sale. These programs are not cheap, but they are worth every penny in the long run.

When one uses a scanner, the items to be scanned are placed onto a glass plate that looks like that of a photocopier, and the mouse's button for "scan" is pressed to start the process. Aside from turning the paper over and scanning the other side, there is nothing left to do with the scanner except turn it on and off. It is a complicated device in the technical aspect, but simple to use in its application. I cannot provide any more instructions about its use, except to advise cleaning the glass with care.

The printer requires very little in the operation area aside from turning it on and putting the correct cartridge in it when printing checks and engaging in other magnetic-ink projects. It is pretty much self-controlling, and the functions that are controlled will be operated through the PC and software. One good thing about the HPIII is that it has a self-check for problems. It will tell the user if it has a problem, and, most likely, how to fix it. It will probably be compatible with the forger's system, since it is a very common office machine and is designed to be plugged in and turned on for instant use. When it comes time to create checks, there will be a need for additional information to be put into the printer's memory. The funny-looking letters and numbers that run along the bottoms of checks and some other bank documents are printed with magnetic ink in special "fonts." Fonts are special characters and can be found in several "business font" programs which are sold at computer stores. One should be specific when buying these, because only certain ones will work on checks. If the forger tells the salesman that business fonts are needed for check printing, he will be able to help. I have had a hard time in the past trying to find such programs on my own, so I call a few places before I drive around. They usually come in a package with a couple of hundred other fonts, and most people will not know what is being requested, so one shouldn't be surprised when a salesman displays a blank expression. The specific term for these needs is *Magnetic Encryption Character Fonts*, but good luck passing that term off on a salesman! The forger will also need the MICR for check printing. These run about $75 at most cartridge-recycling places, and are used all of the time in the printing field. If a customer asks for one by name, few salesmen will notice or care about the request. One cartridge goes a long way, and they have a long shelf life. *NOTE: 1. One should always remove the cartridge when moving the printer. Toner powder can spill from the cartridge and get into all sorts of places where it doesn't belong. 2. The MICR fonts are E13B and CMC7. E13B is used in North and Central America and CMC7 is used in South America and Europe with some exceptions.*

There is no universal electronic MICR font sets that will optimally work in all MICR laser printers. So you would have to buy a set of fonts designed for whichever printer you own.

Optically read check processing fonts are OCR-A and OCR-B. These are mainly used in European countries.

Additional help can be solicited from most computer stores by just telling them what is needed. The on-demand printing business is a growing field, and there is no reason for a supplier to question a prospective customer's intentions. It is not illegal to acquire or possess this knowledge, and the forger will just be scanning and changing paperwork anyway. The tools purchased will actually be overkill for what is needed, but there is no other way to get what is required for top-notch forgeries. Just because the setup can do so much more doesn't mean that the salesman, or any other instructor who might be hired to train the forger, needs to be told what is actually going to be done with the equipment. I have found that if one acts as if one has a person who knows computers in his employ, one can ask dumb questions and not appear to be stupid. Remember, the forger will have a setup that is probably more expensive than the salesman or instructor has, so it is not a bad idea to realize this and act as if he is not the main user of the equipment and software. Once the forger has spent a few days playing with his new toy, the potential for future forgeries grows greater as his skill level climbs. Keep in mind that the forger does not have to try to use any document that does not meet with his satisfaction. The forger will have the original to compare his work to. The forger has all the time it takes to make the end product come out perfect. The law is only broken if (or when) the forger passes (or attempts to pass) forged documents as authentic ones. The beauty of this type of work is that the forger can take enough time to do it right. If the forger is curious as to the latest techniques used to defeat the type of fraud being perpetrated, he can just call any bank and tell them that he is trying to protect his business from such a fraud. The bank will usually supply a current copy of the industry's pamphlet on the subject. The system can be used to work for crime, conversely to the way banks intend it to be used. They spend millions of dollars a year on countermeasures. All the forger need do is ask for their information in a believable guise, and it will be forthcoming. These types of crimes, and the methods employed to counteract them, are always increasing and undergoing refinements, and it is up to the professional criminal to stay abreast of current developments. An ounce of precaution is worth a pound of cure. In this instance, ten minutes of preparation and research are well worth ten years of "rehabilitation" in the slammer on down the line.

List of Relevant Terms:

- CORELDRAW – Software program used for creating and changing documents
- FONT – Term used for describing characters in printing.
- MICR cartridge – The magnetic-ink character recognition cartridge required for checks.
- QUICKEN – Software program used for payroll and check creation.
- RAM – Random access memory is the real "thinking space" of a computer. Without enough RAM, some files or programs won't open or run correctly.

- WINDOWS – Software program used for running other programs.

There is an incredible amount of info at:

http://www.xeroxmicr.com/micr101.html

and at:

http://www.sensible-solutions.com/micr.html

Printers for which MICR cartridges are available:
Printer Model: Hewlett Packard 5Si
Printer Model: Hewlett Packard 4, 4+, 5
Printer Model: Hewlett Packard 5P
Printer Model: Hewlett Packard 4L, 4P
Printer Model: Hewlett Packard 3Si, 4Si
Printer Model: Hewlett Packard II, III, IID, IIID
Printer Model: Hewlett Packard IIp, IIIp
Printer Model: Hewlett Packard 4V
Printer Model: IBM 4019, 4028, 4029
Printer Model: IBM 4039, 4049, Optra Series
Printer Model: Epson 6000, Toshiba Pagelaser 6
Printer Model: NEC 800/900
Printer Model: Panasonic KXP-4420
Printer Model: Pentax LaserFold 240
Printer Model: Okidata 400/800 (Not 400e)
Printer Model: TI OmniLaser 2150
Printer Model: Ricoh 4080, 4081, 4150
Printer Model: TI Microlaser +
Printer Model: Sharp 9500
Printer Model: Brother 630s
ST MICR Lexmark
OTC Continuous Laser Printers

14

The following printers require the installation of a SIMM chip to support MICR. The SIMM includes the fonts and some utilities for security, etc.

HP LaserJet 6P, 6MP

HP LaserJet 5, 5N, 5M

HP LaserJet 5Si, 5Si/MX.

Chapter Four

The Notary Stamp

Another piece of business equipment that is useful is a *notary stamp* or *seal*. There are some types of documents which require this form of authenticity to make them acceptable in normal usage. It is a reflection of the naïveté of our sheeplike society that such a simple thing can instill a sense of security in the mind of the observer. If one were to put a notary stamp on a piece of used toilet paper, the large number of people who would accept it as a legal document would be laughable. I suggest no such deception, however. I notarize only authentic-looking documents, and try not to smile too broadly when they are accepted by the professional men and women who are their intended recipients.

The real secret to acquiring a notary stamp is to ask for it. Since most people don't, they incorrectly assume that it is hard to obtain, and do without it. Every office-supply store in the U.S.A. carries them or can direct the seeker to someplace else that does. Mail box services sell them, as do a host of other places one can find in the telephone directory. If one takes the notarized portion of *any* document that bears any version of the embossing-type seal most commonly used and accepted these days, or a photocopy of it into one of these places, they can usually have the stamp or seal ready in less than 24 hours.

16

It is actually just for comparison or ease of explanation to the sales clerk. You know, a picture is worth a thousand words type of deal. Plus, it shows the person that you are in possession of what you want to have made because you want another one or you have lost the original and simply want an exact duplicate. It really comes down to just making it quick and easy on the salesperson., who most times is tickled to have a picture to go with her order since they usually subcontract out such work, and a picture is the best way to insure the final product. The key is to act like you simply are doing a normal thing that you have done before. Or, that you are simply doing this for a busy friend... this way reduces answering questions you might not want to answer. Remember, if you encounter any resistance or feel you don't like the setup, just go to one of the many other places that do the same thing, or contact a service that actually runs errands for you for a fee. This is not against the law for the most part, and few will question you doing it if you dress and act the part of the professional you are supposed to be portraying.

The application for a notary seal is available in most places for the asking, but it is not necessary for the purchase of one, it only "sometimes" facilitates the process, if the forger wishes to imply that they are new and unfamiliar with the process. If you play dumb and try it at one or two places, when you approach the third place, you should be a pro at the small talk required.

In some states, the application can be made directly to the Department of Licensing. The forger can call and inquire, or he can politely ask a notary what the procedure for obtaining a seal is, and then follow his or her instructions.

The professional forger usually prefers the embossing type of notary seal to the stamp type. It is much more official-looking, and is used more often on the sorts of documents upon which I will be expounding. One doesn't have to show any particular type of notary identification in order to buy it. I don't think that there is any such thing, and I have never been asked for any. If the forger states that he is a notary, who is going to challenge that assertion?

Certainly not an office-supply store employee, whose job is to assist, not harass, the customer.

STATE OF WASHINGTON
Department of
Licensing

BUSINESS AND PROFESSIONS DIVISION
NOTARY PUBLIC SECTION
P.O. BOX 9027
OLYMPIA, WA 98507-9027

APPLICATION FOR APPOINTMENT OR REAPPOINTMENT AS A

FOR VALIDATION ONLY

NOTARY PUBLIC

FEE: $20.00 Make remittance payable to: WASHINGTON STATE TREASURER

PLEASE TYPE OR PRINT CLEARLY

001-000-256-0001

APPLICANT INFORMATION ☐ **Original application** ☐ **Renewal**

Applicant Name _____
PRINT OR TYPE NAME EXACTLY AS YOUR OFFICIAL SIGNATURE IS TO APPEAR ON THE NOTARY SEAL/STAMP

Address _____
PO BOX/STREET

City _____ State _____ Zip Code _____ County _____

Telephone number (_____) _____
DURING NORMAL BUSINESS HOURS
☐ WA Resident ☐ Non-resident, State _____

Date of Birth _____/_____/_____ Sex ☐ M ☐ F Currently employed by the state of Washington? ☐ Yes ☐ No
MO. DAY YR.

Previous appointment date; name and license reference number: _____

ENDORSER SIGNATURES

I, the undersigned endorser, being a person eligible to vote in the state of Washington, and of the age of 18 or more, believe the applicant for a notary public appointment, who is not related to me, to be a person of integrity and good moral character and capable of performing notarial acts.

1. _____ _____ _____
   ENDORSER'S SIGNATURE   ADDRESS, CITY, STATE, ZIP   DATE OF SIGNING
2. _____ _____ _____
   ENDORSER'S SIGNATURE   ADDRESS, CITY, STATE, ZIP   DATE OF SIGNING
3. _____ _____ _____
   ENDORSER'S SIGNATURE   ADDRESS, CITY, STATE, ZIP   DATE OF SIGNING

FOR OFFICE USE ONLY

Comments: _____

CERT DATE _____

CERT NO. _____

Notary application forms are different in every state.
An applicant in Washington State must fill out this two-page form.

Document Fraud And Other Crimes Of Deception

18

APPLICANT PERSONAL DATA

1. Have you been convicted of a crime, misdemeanor or felony in this state, any other state, by the federal government, or any other jurisdiction within the past ten years? ☐ Yes ☐ No

2. Is there a criminal complaint, accusation, or information presently pending against you or are you currently under indictment in this state, any other state, by the federal government, or any other jurisdiction? ☐ Yes ☐ No

3. Has any professional or occupational license, certification, or permit held by you, been fined, suspended, revoked, refused or denied in this state, any other state, by the federal government or any other jurisdiction? ☐ Yes ☐ No

4. Have you ever had a civil court order, verdict, or judgment entered against you in any court of competent jurisdiction in this state, any other state, by the federal government, or any other jurisdiction? ☐ Yes ☐ No

Please attach a letter of explanation for any affirmative answers to the above questions, including charge(s), date of conviction, civil judgement or order, county jurisdiction, state, and disposition of charges.

DECLARATION OF APPLICANT

I, _____, solemnly swear or affirm under penalty of
　　　　　　　　　　　　　　PRINT NAME

perjury that the personal information I have provided in this application is true, complete, and correct; that I have carefully read the materials provided describing the duties of a notary public in and for the state of Washington; and, that I will perform to the best of my ability, all notarial acts in accordance with the law. I have carefully read the questions in the foregoing application and have answered them completely, and pursuant to RCW 9A.72.085, I declare under penalty of perjury under the law of the state of Washington that my answers and all statements made by me herein are true and correct. Should I furnish any false information in this application, I hereby agree that such act shall constitute cause for the denial, suspension or revocation of my appointment as a notary public in the state of Washington.

_____
SIGNATURE OF APPLICANT　　　　　　　　　　　　　　　DATE

_____
CITY　　　　　　　　　　　　　　　　　　　　　　STATE

Signed and sworn to before me on this_____day of _____, 19_____

_____
COUNTY AND STATE

SEAL

_____
SIGNATURE OF NOTARY PUBLIC

_____
PRINTED NAME OF NOTARY PUBLIC

_____
RESIDING AT

_____
EXPIRATION DATE OF NOTARY PUBLIC APPOINTMENT

UPON FILING, THIS APPLICATION BECOMES A PUBLIC RECORD AND IS SUBJECT TO PUBLIC DISCLOSURE PROVISIONS PURSUANT TO RCW 42.17.

Page 2 of Notary application.

The forger need merely pick up several applications and fill them out with different information, then drop them off at several office-supply emporiums and see what happens. If accosted, he is just a messenger doing his job, or a person doing a favor for a friend. It is best to have several different notary seals anyway, in case there is a need for several pieces of notarized paperwork to be used at the same place.

It is helpful to use the words "state"- or "county"-something when obtaining notary seals, such as "Clark County Developers" or "Southern Nevada State Planning Company." The object here is to create the impression, for the person looking at the notarized document, that it is official. If they see the words "state" or "county" on it when they look at the already-hard-to-see impression, they will most likely accept it as legitimate.

Manipulate the seal with a computer if you can, or simply use one as an example of the way you want yours to appear. The round-impression types are actually pretty restrictive in their layout due to obvious reasons, and the desire to have one made from another's layout is an easy explanation, and makes sense too. Remember, they are a service that makes what the customer wants them to, and most often their employees view the customer as someone they wish to please, so act like you are doing one of the thousand other things you do regularly, and you'll be fine.

This is a game of illusion, and the forger must never stop practicing it, even when it looks like there is no need for it. Before long, it becomes second nature, and when one least expects it, a small, faintly-steaming portion of bullshit will save the day. The words on the notary seal are not critical, but why not cover as many bases as possible? It requires so little effort to do the job correctly, and I can't see doing it any other way.

It doesn't matter which state the forger obtains the notary seals in, as they are accepted everywhere in the country. I have never been asked a single question concerning the seals on any of the documents I have passed as legitimate, and they number in the hundreds. One should keep in mind, in case one is asked, that the document was notarized by someone whose name came from a telephone directory, or someone who was met at an unremembered place of business, or perhaps someone who advertised via a sign at the side of the road with their telephone number on it. How much does anyone really remember about any notary whom they have used before?

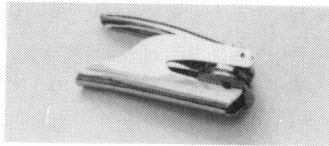

The embossing-type of notary seal has been in use for many years. The forger often uses this kind of a seal.

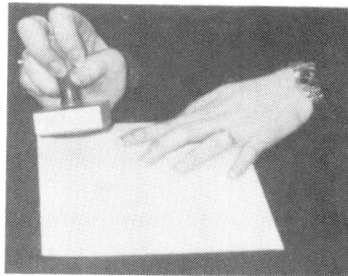

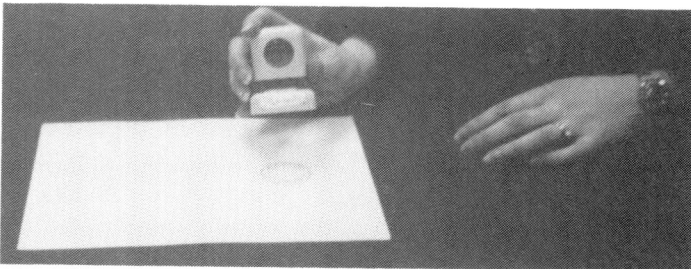

Notary seals are also available as stamps, either traditional (above) or pre-inked (below).

Only a small percentage of the work that a forger does will require a seal anyway, but I covered it because it is an important tool that all aspiring document defrauders have at their disposal. Besides, a notary seal will come in handy more often than might be imagined. Since the part of the document that the seal is affixed to requires one to inscribe the expiration date of the seal next to it, any date desired can be entered, and it will last forever. I do, however, change seals every year or two. They are easy to get, and one does not want to leave a trail if it can be avoided.

NOTE: This device comes in very handy in the fake ID department, as well as when selling stolen cars.

The knowledgeable forger takes advantage of the services dispensed by the National Notary Association (NNA) by calling its national office at (818)713-4000. This organization offers a home-study course that provides in-depth information about the services that a notary public can and cannot provide. The NNA publishes *The National Notary Magazine*, whose editors have prepared notary law primers for several states. Memberships cost $29 per year, and members are entitled to discounts on NNA products. Catalogs are free. NNA publications are often found in public libraries.

Chapter Five

Putting It All Together

The next step is assembling all of the new toys and making them do the job for which they are intended. If there is no budget crisis, I rent an office to work out of somewhere. One can find an *"Executive Suite,"* or other small office space, for a few hundred bucks a month in most cities. Renting one allows the forger to both run an operation and have a social life that doesn't have to be kept out of a certain room, or necessitate lying about why he has such a serious array of computer equipment sitting at home. Most people don't, and it attracts attention. The forger can tell all of the stories he wants to, but curiosity is a dangerous thing. Besides, getting up and going to a workplace as if one has a real job answers a lot of questions that nosy people routinely ask about the non-working person who appears to live pretty well. Going to the office also puts the forger into the work mode! After all, this is a job, not a hobby. If someone is coming in to explain certain applications on the computer, or there are phone calls or mail that is business-related, an office is a necessary cover and a place whose location only the forger and those he chooses to meet there need know.

If the forger is doing the smart thing by living and creating the product in one city and going to another city to generate revenue, an office and a self-employed appearance allow him to offer any explanations that may be necessary in order to demonstrate his legitimate livelihood. It is assumed that most people work for a living, so if the forger intends to pass more or less unnoticed, he must play the game a little and fabricate a false front.

Crime has always been the easy part of any adventure. The real test of a survivor is his ability to blend in and pass the "normal person" test. An office is also desirable because it restricts the number of people who might *accidentally* get a look at the projects in development. People are basically asleep, but even a drowsy person knows what official-looking stuff is, and the paper and other materials on hand definitely qualify as official-looking stuff. Most offices have plenty of business-related things lying about; this always happens, no matter how hard one tries to keep it tidy. Relationships may come and go, but if knowledge of the business at hand goes with them, this creates liabilities that can come back to haunt one later. Most of the materials the forger works with will look office-related if seen in a workplace, but rather strange at home. Remember, this is not a one-time score, but an ongoing criminal enterprise. Certain rules must be applied to one's lifestyle and practices. The forger is going to be coming and going fairly regularly, and will sometimes be gone for several weeks at a time. He must consider the possibility that someone might get a peek at the setup without his knowledge or permission. The forger should never give anyone permission to look at anything that he is doing, unless he is naïve enough to believe that they will keep it a secret forever. If the gear and paperwork are kept in an office environment, they will most likely appear to be normal and, therefore, be ignored. Unfortunately, the family and friends in our lives whom we choose to trust cannot be counted on to keep their noses out of our private places and affairs. If a person is gone, and people know the time frame, I will bet a Ferrari that they will snoop. No one can be sure enough to bet against me. Our prying loved ones will convince themselves that they can talk their way out of it if caught. Besides, they are *loved*, and most people consider being loved a license to do anything (and most do). Just reflect back on your life for a moment, and you will see my point. It began with your parents going through your pockets, and it will end with the mortician doing the same thing.

Chapter Six

Getting Started

The steps are pretty straightforward, and the forger should soon receive the starter package from one of the paper suppliers. If this does not happen in a timely fashion, the forger simply orders a variety of stock so that he will have some practice with different types of documents. Most of the documents used today follow some basic formats, so the stock is often already cut to size or has perforations in the correct places. Often, there will be industry-accepted printing already on the paper which is ordered, such as: a border on certificates or blank checks; the words *"Sign Here"* or *"Endorse Here"*; and a line for the actual signing of some of the names that are expected to be written on these documents. When one buys the paper to forge payroll checks, it will come in sheets like those which banks provide when business accounts are opened. There will be a certain amount of checks per page, and the borders and perforations between each check on the page will already be there. All the forger has to do is add the rest of the information, and the procedure is finished. The reason a lot of paper comes this way is because the information printed on the backside of a document is standardized, and the only personalized printing needed will be on the frontside. This reduces the amount of time it takes to print payroll checks, and eliminates the need to print on both sides of the paper. In some cases, the name or logo of the paper manufacturer will appear in small print in the corners or along the borders. This is common, so the forger will see different ones as he receives and inspects authentic documents. It's no different than the various mint designations that appear on money, so there is no need to worry about it. Size and shape are also pretty much standardized, and are already prepared for the forger by the manufacturer.

Toner (ink) is all pretty much the same color, so all of the forger's needs will be covered by a normal toner cartridge. When the forger creates checks (or other documents that need the magnetic ink toner), all he does is switch cartridges in the printer and keep on going. He can even print the entire check with the magnetic ink. It is identical to regular toner, except that it has magnetic particles in it which cannot be seen with the naked eye. There will come a time when the forger considers making documents that require color. These are not much different than any of the other items he will be creating, and aside from the colored parts, they will be printed in the same way. Until that time, the colored parts of the documents can be printed by any local print shop. This is what they do for a living, and the forger is just another customer unless he acts differently. The idea is to get the colored parts printed first, so there is really no way for the print shop's employees to know what the finished product will look like. Partial printing is done all of the time by these places and it is not a big or costly deal.

The forger can purchase a color printer to do the color printing himself, but should keep in mind that an InkJet printer is not a LaserJet printer, and won't be adequate. The difference in results is too great for the forger to use anything but a LaserJet for color printing, so it is a lot easier to just take a certificate to a printer and have him do the work one wants done. Another big difference is cost. A decent color laser printer is almost five or six thousand dollars more than an InkJet. The forger can avoid color if so desired, and it will not cost much in lost illicit gains, but the desire to use color will eventually present itself, so at least he should know the method to use.

Most of the paper the forger will work with can be ordered in the required colors. Black ink is the standard, so the forger should stick to what can be purchased already finished, until he is ready to experiment and waste a little time and money. There is more of a challenge in doing difficult jobs, and it can be a good motivator to get to the next skill level. There will be plenty to keep the forger busy, and there will also be an occasional setback. There will be no situation that cannot be solved by using one's head and some creative talking, so the forger should look forward to the task, and be ready when it arrives. There is no one to contradict the forger or his actions, so he can offer any credible explanation and it will probably be accepted. No one will know what the forger is creating, as long as he acts like a normal customer. If the forger complains about shoddy work, he can expect the same response as any other customer. None of the many documents floating around out there are particularly hard to reproduce (with the exception of cash, which is made on very unique paper). Once a forger has followed these procedures and fabricated documents a few times, it becomes readily apparent how simple the process really is.

What is really needed is some practice and a few easy-to-get documents to work with. The forger can start with a birth certificate and some car titles. He need merely order a clean copy of the title to his own vehicle from his state's Department of Motor Vehicles, or his birth certificate from the Vital Statistics Office of the state in which he was born. The documents will not be used in their original form, so the forger can start with his own or a friend's. Once the forger has scanned the format into the computer, any necessary information can be deleted or changed. The forger should use new, or at least wrinkle-free, paperwork to copy from, because the scanner will pick up the smallest imperfections and reproduce them on the duplicate. When a document is scanned into the computer, the forger should not forget to do the backside as well as the front. It is often necessary to do both, and all that is required is putting the paper back into the scanner, only upside down the second time. This will take a little getting used to, but practice makes perfect. The forger will be using the cut-and-paste process on the computer when working on the documents, so he must remember never to change the original copy. He just makes additional copies of the original file to work on (and make mistakes with). Once the forger has what he considers to be the right setup on the screen, then he simply prints it and sees how close he is to getting it right. A light table will allow the forger to place one copy on top of the original to see how to align it correctly, but it can also just be held up to any light. Once again, it's the forger's project, so he must do what he wants to in the equipment department.

It is nearly impossible to thoroughly describe the complete process, since each computer, or set of programs that are being worked with, will be different. The forger can follow the computer's instructions, and it will take him through the steps better than the instructions in this book ever could. The forger can make all of the mistakes he wants to on a computer screen, since it is easy to delete any imperfections that aren't desired before the final copy is printed. Most systems today have a "help" program already built into them. All one needs to do to ask for help is to place the mouse's arrow (the cursor) on the *Help* indicator and click the button (just as is done for all of the other functions). This may seem complicated, but it really isn't. By the time the forger is at this stage of the work, he will already know how to do this. If the forger still needs some assistance or explanations, he can call a computer store or service and ask for guidance. A professional computer trainer will be glad to come over and provide one-on-one instruction, for money of course. The newspapers and specialized local computer-oriented publications are full of ads from individuals and businesses offering this service, and they will show the forger how to properly operate the equipment. Nothing that the forger is doing will seem out of the ordinary, if he tells the trainer that his intention is to open a desktop publishing service. If the instructor knows this up front, the forger can call and ask for further assistance in the future, and the trainer will already know his needs and be able to help over the phone. The forger should definitely develop some type of rapport with an instructor or knowledgeable person, so that help is available for future projects when needed. If the trainer comes to visit the forger and examines the computer firsthand, the forger can more easily learn how to do what is wanted on the setup at hand. This is another reason why an office is a good investment. The forger should practice with these documents until he is satisfied with the results, and then it's his ballgame.

The forger can try some stocks and bonds for the minimal cost of some low-value paperwork. Most stocks and bonds are printed on the same type of paper, so the forger practices with the cheap stuff to see if he is capable of fabricating false documents, and whether or not he is truly interested in this line of business. In reality, it is simple to forge almost all of the documents currently in circulation, but the forger should choose documents that meet specific needs. That should be kept in mind as the forger practices his trade. There are more specific details as to the actual duplicating and use of documents in a later chapter, but at this stage in his development the forger needs to learn how to do these procedures until his work is acceptable and usable. If it takes the forger more than a week or two to attain the needed skill level, something is wrong. The processes of this trade should all be picked up in a day or two. Forgery isn't all that hard to learn. Tuning up a car is more difficult!

The forger can receive instructions on how to operate
his computer in the privacy of his office.

Chapter Seven

Checks

If one intends to make money in this business, then one can get started by mastering the creation of realistic-looking checks, or the *"rubber check scam,"* which is relatively easy to do. This is the perfect place for the fledgling forger to start. The learning is quick, and the payoff is good. I will skip discussing personal checks; they have little value unless the forger wants to improve his wardrobe or perhaps buy some trinkets. This is generally inadvisable, as it shows his face to a lot of people who will probably have to pay for the bad checks they accept. Most likely they would be minimum-wage working stiffs who haven't got a chance in this world anyway, so the altruistic forger should give them a break and stick to more impersonal targets, such as banks and the cash they provide.

Millions of payroll checks are cashed every week, and no matter what the opposition does to discourage the creation of fraudulent imitations, they are still the best game in town for quick cash. Payroll checks and refund checks, both of which are easy to get and to work with, will be discussed later in this chapter. There are a few things that are consistent in this type of work, and the process will be reviewed to make sure that they are understood. There are always variations, but some things remain the same, and it's those constants that will be discussed.

The first thing is cashing the checks. In order to cash as many as possible, the forger must first set up the places ahead of time. Local supermarkets and bars will cash some of the checks, but the majority of them will be cashed at the branches of the bank where the perpetrator has opened accounts. When the forger intends to do this work in a particular city, he must first open up as many accounts as needed at different banks around town. Different names can be used if so desired, but unless the forger intends to make this more than a one-day affair, a single name will usually suffice. If the forger plans to complete the work over a period of several days, using multiple bank accounts, then two or three names should be used. That sort of planning is for an advanced job, and for now I will be explaining the single-day version. The advanced version will be easily understood once the basics are covered and the process has been fully explained. When the forger cashes the checks, he will be going into the bank and simply depositing some of the money into his own account and then walking out with the difference. The forger will be doing this in as many bank branches as time and distance will allow. It will take one business day to accomplish this task, and that is the time frame that needs to be considered when the forger lays out the route he will take from branch to branch. I use a map of the city and a well-planned route. After all, time is money.

When the forger opens up accounts at the various bank branches, he will need to deposit at least a grand into each checking account. This will allow the cashier to look at the forger's balance when he is cashing checks, and ascertain that the check will be covered if it does not clear the other bank. This is what the cashier looks at when a customer's account information is displayed on the computer screen while he is standing there waiting for his money.

One thing to be aware of is that if the bank puts a hold on the forger's account while it waits for the other check to clear, the forger will not be able to cash any more checks in that bank's system. The forger is screwed if he does not have another backup bank system to fall back on. This can be prevented from happening, and it's important that this matter be handled correctly. The cashier will do her thing, and then she will inform the forger that she will have to put a hold on the check until it clears the bank it is drawn on. This is a normal banking occurrence, and is not a cause for alarm. It is then that the forger informs the cashier that he does not want any holds put on that account, and because of that will just go to the bank that the check is drawn on and get it cashed there. The forger acts friendly while saying this, and it seems normal to the cashier. She will be glad to accommodate this request, and will hand back the check. *The forger must never leave the bank without the check or cash,* unless finished with the scam.

Another thing to be aware of when opening up a New Account is that the New Accounts representative will call a service that supplies information to the banking industry concerning new-account requests. Through them, the New Accounts representative will verify that the new depositor did not leave any other banks hanging with bad checks or other debts. This is not a problem for the forger, because he will be using ID that has never been used before while conducting business. This is the phone call that the New Accounts representative always makes while the new depositor is opening up the account. The bank has no way of verifying the Social Security number that the new depositor is using, as this service only uses its database for checking on new accounts. If the information that the new depositor is supplying is not in the service's database, it will say "OK."

One problem that might arise is easily dealt with. It will come in the form of the New Accounts representative informing the forger that she has been told by the Veri-Check service that he has opened up another account at a different bank that day or the preceding day. If this happens, the forger simply informs her that the other account is a joint account with a lover or housemate, and that he wants a separate one for himself. This makes sense, and it answers the question that the New Accounts representative is required to ask whenever this sort of situation arises with anyone who wants to open a new account. It is her job to ask the new depositor to explain the situation, and once she has an answer that makes sense, her job is done and she moves on. It is her job to open up new accounts, not chase off potential customers, so the forger should relax and be ready for the question if it is asked.

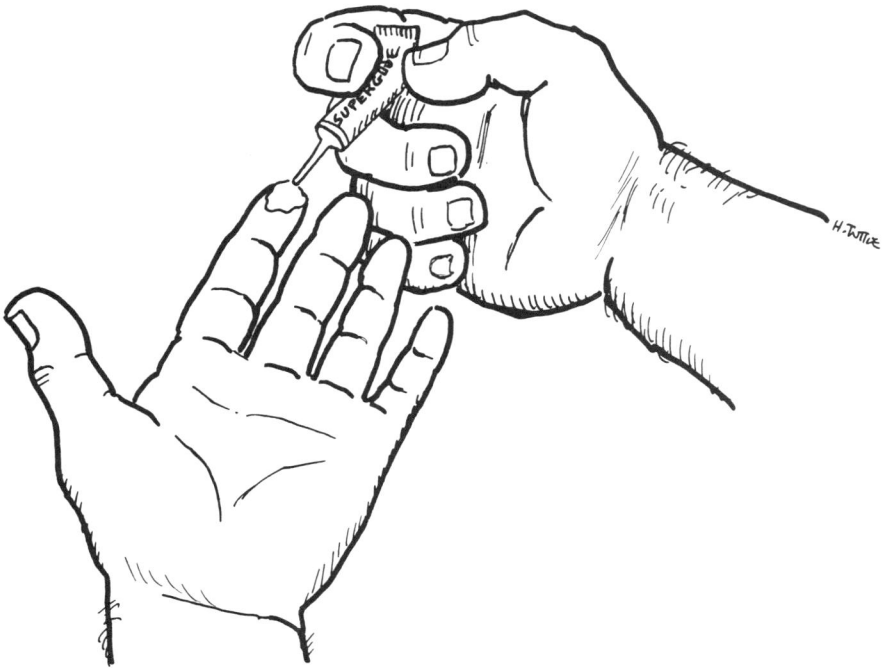

*The forger sometimes obfuscates his fingerprints
by applying super glue to his fingertips.*

Another important point to remember is that law enforcement can get fingerprints off of a check with very little effort. Each time the forger handles a check or deposit slip, he is leaving his prints all over them, and fingerprints stay on paper for a long, long time. This also holds true for all of the documents that the forger will be handling in his other endeavors. The forger must never forget that the other team has vast technology and resources, and to remain free he must practice self-protection at all levels of his business. A rough physical description or poor-quality photographs are very little to go on, and most banks won't even have that to supply to investigators. If the forger cannot wear gloves, which in most cases is not an option, then fingerprints must be covered or altered in another way. A simple trick that has been used for years and never fails is to put super glue on the swirl of the fingerprint of each finger. Super glue is durable, and when used in moderation is almost invisible. It is unlikely that anyone will see it on the forger's fingers, and it will stay there until he decides to take it off. These two aspects of the glue make it an ideal method of eliminating this threat to the forger's success and freedom. Some brands work better than others, so the forger should find one that works for him and get a supply of it for his crime kit, as altering fingerprints is a precautionary measure that should be taken all of the time.

All checks are intended to be read by a magnetic reader at some point. When a forger prints his own checks, he must print them with an MICR in the printer. It is a must, and only a fool would not use it and then try to pass the checks. One can print the entire check with the magnetic cartridge, since the magnetic ink and regular toner are the same color and it is difficult to tell the difference between them. When the cashier takes the check from the forger at the bank counter, she runs it through a small device called a reader. This device scans the information on the bottom of the check and transfers that information to the computer screen in front of her. This is a time-saving device, but it is also a security device. When it doesn't work for her, she will enter the information by hand, but a red flag has been raised in her head. She will continue to service the customer, but a signal has been given to someone else by a key stroke she made that the customer did not see her make. The forger can usually talk his way out of these situations, because the check is not reported stolen or missing and everything looks normal, but I would not want to make myself known to the bank personnel for the few dollars at stake. It's the danger of this sort of confrontation that makes using stolen or poorly printed checks a bad idea.

There is a handy device that makes check fraud a little easier. This device is called a check protector or check writer, and it is the machine used to emboss the amount of the check in color across the *"Amount"* section of the document. Most people have seen a check embossed this way before. Checks that are embossed in this manner are more readily accepted in the banking world than those that are not. It's mostly hocus-pocus, but it works very well, and that is all that really matters in this game. One brand name is *Paymaster*. New ones can be purchased at most office-supply places, and used ones can often be found at second-hand office-equipment stores. They run about $150 new, but used they cost much less. Unlike the paper and the printer, a check protector leaves an embossment that is unique to the machine, so the forger gets a new one for each city that he does work in. That way he does not leave a trail.

Computer-generated signatures are very common these days, so the forger creates a file in his computer's memory for saving any official-looking signatures he comes across. He just scans and saves them for later use. It doesn't matter which name is used in the signature space, as he will never be cashing checks at the bank that they are drawn on, and there is never anything to try to match. The whole idea is to make the checks look as professionally prepared as possible. The forger is going to be dealing with checks which are drawn for large amounts of money, so there is a certain amount of scrutiny to be expected.

There are various ways to carry out check fraud, and the first one that comes to mind requires nothing more than opening a business account at a bank and then cashing the checks the bank provides at different banks as if they were the forger's own paychecks. This method works fine, and it has only a few restrictions. They are few, but very important. I do not do this type of crime any more, but I used to and I never got caught, so I guess that makes me an expert on the subject. There are a few items that the forger needs to deal with in this particular scam, and it can be done with great success once the concept is understood.

This scam has a realistic limit to the amount of funds it can return: about ten or fifteen thousand dollars. This is by no means chump change, but it can be multiplied many times with a little planning and a reasonable investment of time and money. It can be tried as a confidence-builder, but the second method, discussed later, is better-suited to making bigger money with less risk or hassle.

1. When the forger opens the account, he deposits at least a grand, but not much more than two. Since it will be in cash, too much will look suspicious.

2. A business license is not always required, but since they are easy to get and cost little, having one enables the forger to carry out this crime correctly and with fewer questions.

3. The forger must insist that the check numbers be started above 1000. This is essential in the cashing of them, as low numbers reflect a new account to those who know checks. If the forger tells the New Accounts representative that he wants them because he has been writing checks already for his business and does not want duplicate numbers, she will accept that as a valid request and usually grant it. If not, go to a bank that will.

4. The forger will name his company something professional sounding. It will not matter to the bank, but it will matter to the person cashing the check. *Colorado Professional Services* sure sounds better than *Bob's Jobs*, doesn't it? Impression is everything.

5. The forger will never cash the checks at the bank or branches his account is with, until he is ready to get his initial deposit back and end the scam.

6. The forger tells the New Accounts representative that he prefers to pick up his new checks at the bank instead of having them mailed to him.

7. The forger uses the address of an existing vacant building or a mail box for his business address. Bank personnel often know the city well enough to know the address he might use, so making one up is a mistake.

8. A cellular phone is cheap and worth the cost. They can be rented with a small deposit. The bank will call the forger's business number with a lame excuse, but it is really a verification tool that is used for checking up on him. The forger answers as if it were a business, or uses a voice-messaging service, but a phone the bank can reach him at is a must. Plus, if there is a routine problem, the bank will always start the research with a call to the forger. This is an early-warning device that can keep the forger out of jail, so he considers it cheap insurance.

9. This scam has a one business-day life span, so it doesn't pay to get greedy.

10. If possible, the forger uses a bank that lets him bank by phone or issues an ATM card to make deposits and check balances. A business account usually does not let the forger withdraw funds from it, but the card and phone functions allow him to make periodic checks on his account throughout the day, so that he can see that everything is OK with his account and ensure that it is safe to enter another bank. Plus, some of the deposits the forger will be making as he cashes checks will be credited to his account, and his balance will increase. If the forger's balance has increased to the point where he will be satisfied to withdraw it and call it a day, then he should get a cashier's check and exchange it at a coin shop for gold that can be converted back into cash later. This allows him to get a large amount out of the account at one time in a normal fashion. If the ATM machine keeps the forger's card, or a telephone call asks him to talk to a bank representative to straighten out an account problem, the scam is over and the banks are the last place he wants to be.

(Some bars and supermarkets will cash smaller checks after the banks close, but the forger shouldn't expect a great deal of success with this ploy.)

If the forger doesn't want to open his own business just to get some checks, he can steal some from an existing business. This is not recommended, but it is an alternative to getting them directly from the bank that can be utilized in an emergency.

If the forger-cum-burglar does choose to get some checks from an existing business, there are a few things that might make the deed go a little easier. First off, he shouldn't take them from the checkbook, but should instead take the extras that are kept in a box from the bank. If the forger does take checks from the checkbook, he should take ones from the bottom of the pad, which will hopefully not be missed for a while. The forger can still cash such checks at his bank, but if the bank calls the business to verify funds, they will most likely be reported stolen, and the scam could end before it begins. The forger can act like a bank and just call up the bank the stolen checks are drawn on, and find out whether the check will clear or not. If the bank says it will clear, the forger knows the checks have not been reported as stolen at that time. This is not a real good way to conduct check fraud, and the penalties are the same for the bad scams as the good ones. If the forger wants to do a scam that uses existing business accounts, then he can use the following method. It is actually a very good way to beat the system, and it's very low-risk.

There are two versions of the following scam, but they differ only in the way the first check is acquired. Once the forger has the master check, the duplicating and cashing are pretty much the same for both of them. In essence, the forger opens accounts at different banks and cashes as many checks as he can in the time allotted. He could do one or both of these; they are easy to do. The forger will need to get a master check for each method. The means to go about duplicating and using them will be discussed next.

The first method requires that the forger obtain a check from a currently open business account. Digging through garbage is a good way to get such a check. If the forger's locksmithing skills are up to par with the rest of his felonious dreams and aspirations, as they should be, then it's really a simple matter to go into a business at night and remove a single check from the back of the master check-book or the boxes of canceled checks that are always around somewhere. He could obtain a canceled check if he has the option. That check will have information on it that can be used to make the forger's work a little more difficult to discover. The forger can delete the portions of the canceled check he does not need when it comes time to work with it. By saving the signature in a file, the forger can use it on the checks he prints later to add a convincing finishing touch. In reality, the signature will mean little, but it is a touch of professionalism that I cannot resist. The forger must keep in mind that this is a lifestyle, not a hobby, and always remember that basic tenet as he struggles to improve his criminal skills.

One of the advantages of burglarizing a business to obtain a master check is that the forger can look at the company checkbook and see what the balance in the company account is. If the forger gets into the office with little or no evidence of his entry, his visit will go unnoticed by the employees. If the forger has to leave traces of his presence, then he can make it look as if his intentions were to do something other than getting a check. If he takes a canceled check and leaves the master checkbook alone, the business has no reason to call the bank concerning the checks. If the forger makes the disturbance look like the work of kids or amateurs, the cops will probably just write it off as petty breaking and entering. If there is a good balance in the checking account, the forger's efforts will be well-rewarded if he covers his tracks.

The forger should focus his efforts on a complex of "Executive Suites" where there will be a number of offices containing checkbooks. His goal should be to find several business accounts with good balances in them, and then setup his operation to make use of those businesses in his scams. The object is to confuse or mislead the police and business owners about his objectives. If the forger removes a canceled check, or one that was in the extra box, he has a grace period of at least a week. He should use that grace time correctly. The "Executive Suites" are easily found in newspapers' classified sections, and most high-rise office buildings have a floor dedicated to them. It is not very expensive to rent one of the suites for a phony business. The forger can even use one of his bad checks, if he rents on a Friday; it will not clear the bank until the following Monday, and if the forger times it right, he can add an extra day by setting up on a holiday weekend. If the forger rents an office, he will be given a set of keys to the building and the alarm setup (if it has an alarm system, as many places do these days). The potential is high for a good score if he rents an office and takes his time going through the other offices. The forger will have many hours to do his job if he goes late at night and leaves in the early hours of the morning. He can get what he wants and be long gone by the time the various businesses in the Executive Suites lurch into action on the next work day. The forger can even call the landlord back and inform him that he has changed his mind and does not wish to rent the office after all. The landlord might bitch, but if the forger did a good job of cleaning up after himself, he need never know that the forger was in the building again after the first time he spoke with him there.

*The forger sometimes resorts to burglary to obtain business checks
(and computer equipment) which are essential to his schemes.*

The above-mentioned method is by far one of the best ways to initiate a check-fraud scam. It allows the forger a chance for a good score, and the risk is quite low in the preparation department. If the forger's locksmithing skills are not as good as he would like them to be, a locked building late at night gives him plenty of practice time and no audience. Even if the forger is a novice at picking locks, he will be surprised at what an hour of undisturbed practice will accomplish. Loompanics Unlimited publishes two excellent books on this subject,

The Complete Guide to Lock Picking and *Home Workshop Professional Lock Tools,* and there are numerous other books, videos, lock-pick kits and devices, and mail-order courses available to the forger who wants to hone his lock picking skills. In addition, it is a good idea for the forger to familiarize himself with the literature on security systems, just to be on the safe side. (Of course, it is always best to get information about these matters from professionals and experts, and if possible, the forger will do this. If incarcerated, he will take advantage of the situation and augment his education in the clandestine arts by learning from acknowledged professionals.)

Most office buildings have suspended-tile ceilings in them, and it is rather simple to lift a tile and enter an adjacent room through the ceiling. A hand-held dustbuster will do a marvelous job of cleaning up the little white particles that drop to the floor when the tiles are removed. They are a dead giveaway that someone has messed with the ceiling, so the forger must make an effort to clean them up if he enters offices in this way.

A second method of obtaining a master check is also very effective. Most people would never even consider this as a method of acquiring checks to do frauds with, and that makes it very desirable and not often thought about or defended against. This is my favorite method of doing check fraud. It is not only virtually risk-free (as far as getting the check), but it also guarantees that the funds in the business account will be sufficient to allow the forger to withdraw all that he wants, and I do mean *all!* I have made over a hundred grand every time I have done this, and with no problems at all. The preparation work is the key, as it usually is in most crimes of intelligence. The forger must take his time on this one, and if he does, his efforts will usually be well-rewarded.

The basic idea is to get a refund check from a local, very recognizable business. Then the forger duplicates it in its original form, and cashes it the same way he would cash any of the other checks he does scams with. The telephone and local utility companies are the best sources for refund checks; they are high-profile, and almost all of the businesses in town will cash their checks for the forger. Once the banks close for the day, the forger can hit supermarkets and bars until they close, too, because the checks actually have to arrive at the bank they are drawn on before they are canceled. If the forger does this scam over a weekend or holiday, he can have several extra days to work with. There are plenty of cities that have 25 or 30 different locations of the same supermarket chain, and probably several different supermarket chains as well. If the forger combines all of these places with the bank branches that are open on Saturday, he will have more places than he can possibly go to as well as plenty of options. Telephone directories will inform the forger which cities are ripe for this kind of opportunity, and if he goes into the supermarkets that he intends to visit later with forged checks, he can usually sign up for some type of program that enables him to cash checks there more smoothly. This is where the planning part of a job is important. The forger can make several years' worth of income in a few days, so it is essential that he take his time and do it right. The penalty for failure, of course, is lengthy incarceration.

Since each of the checks the forger will be cashing will appear to be legally and actually issued, anybody who wishes to inquire as to their validity can do so and receive a verification. When a clerk calls a company about a check, he does not say that the supermarket is cashing the check and that it will be deposited along with the day's receipts. The clerk merely asks if the check is good. The company they are asking simply tells them yes or no, as they do a hundred times a week for all of the other places that call them about other checks. It's unlikely that anyone will call to verify the check, but the forger needn't worry if this happens; it will all be fine.

There are countless ways and places to get checks that will do the job for the forger, but the following are a few of the better ones. Any refund check will do, but the idea is to get big ones, so that the forger's score is as large as his efforts can make it. He can also do this with several smaller checks at the same time. The variations are up to the forger, once he knows what the businesses which cash refund checks expect.

The forger can go to the telephone company and give them the address of a vacant house he saw along the way. He can say that he wants service and all of the options he can think of. The idea is to have them charge the forger as much as possible for installing a telephone, so the forger says that his credit is terrible and he is planning to make lots of long-distance calls. He pays them in cash and hits the door. The forger comes back the next day and informs the telephone company that his arrangements for the house fell through, and that he wants his money back. The telephone company will tell the forger that he will have to take a check, and that it might even take a day or two. The forger doesn't make a big deal out of it, but calmly informs the telephone company that he is living in a hotel until he can find another place, and doesn't want the check mailed. He gets a number to call and a person's name who can tell him when the check is ready for him to pick up. If the forger does the above at a telephone company outlet at a mall, or another business that also sells telephones, he can increase the check amount by buying a phone at the same time he arranges for installation and then just letting them include that refund with the other one. The forger will do what is necessary to obtain the check in the amount he desires. When the forger considers that every dollar that he adds to the refund check will be multiplied by the number of checks he cashes, it is obvious that a little turns into a lot quickly.

The same methodology applies to any refund check the forger wants to do this with. The utility companies are also good places to initiate this process, because they are well-recognized and everyone knows that their checks are good. If the forger has a heart of stone and the balls to match, the IRS refund check is the gold medal of check-fraud crimes. It's more than money when the forger takes it from the government, but so are the ramifications and the payback. There is virtually no way to authenticate a government check, and no place to call and verify its owner anyway. The holes that are cut into them are for later use, so the forger just cuts some with a square-hole cutter (available at any office-supply store) and he's in business. The forger can cash these checks everywhere, and they will probably be paid by the idiots in Washington to boot. The forger can create his own version of a government payroll check if he wants to. These checks have many different formats, and many businesses will cash them. The forger realizes, if he stops to think about it for a moment: How would anyone know that these checks are forgeries? None of the banks will know, as they obligingly cash them for him.

Now that the forger has the master check to work with, he can start the duplication process. It is really no more than just scanning the check into the computer and playing with it until he is satisfied with the results. The paper the forger prints the checks on is not really all that critical, since it is really check paper that he is using, and the color is pretty much standardized. The main objective is to create an authentic-looking check, the numbers on the bottom of it being the most critical detail. The whole process should not take the forger more than a couple of hours to master anyway. The scanner will transfer the company logo and the other details that make the check look authentic and original, but the forger will need to have the computer change the *check numbers* so that each check has a different number on it. The forger's Quicken program should have this feature on it, and he mustn't forget to use it. On a one-day job, or when using refund checks, different numbers won't matter, but if the forger is creating regular payroll checks, the advancing numbers are a must if the scam is planned to run for several days.

Things the Forger Must Remember

- He must be aware of his fingerprints.
- He might be observed entering and exiting his car, so he should keep that in mind when he parks it.
- He must be aware of ATM-machine cameras, and not park within their view.
- He must always check his accounts with the ATM card or via telephone, so that there are no surprises.
- The ATM card might be kept by the machine, so he mustn't let his fingerprints be kept with it.
- He must dress for the part, as this is business.
- A check protector is a major plus in this business, so he must use one.

- The MICR must always be used on checks.
- Mail boxes don't have memories. He must use one, and never have things mailed to a friend's place.
- He mustn't push his luck; there's always another day and another town.
- One final note: The forger needs to make himself aware of the economy in the locale he is working in. This helps him determine the amounts of the checks that he will forge. In places where the economy is strong, the amounts can be larger. The forger must be aware of how the checks appear to the clerks at the banks, markets, bars, and other locations where he cashes checks.

Most banks have what is commonly known as a "teller limit." It almost never exceeds $1,000, and a teller limit of $500 is not uncommon. Checks for larger amounts require a supervisor's approval. A simple phone call made with suavity and decorum can easily establish a bank's teller limit. The forger always stays under that limit.

Tellers ordinarily assume that if a customer is depositing some of the money, the check is legitimate. The forger should act like a business person who is in somewhat of a hurry, yet is polite and friendly. A comment such as, "At last I'm getting that used jet-ski my girlfriend has been asking for!" sometimes greases the wheels ("used" means that cash is required for the transaction). "Forgot my checkbook this morning, so just give me hundreds for most of it, but I will need several hundred in twenties, too!" is also helpful. Tellers deal with dozens of professional people every day, and they see patterns and common characteristics, so the forger must look and act the part if he is out to cash large checks. Otherwise, he should stick to blue-collar-sized checks.

The forger must always act like a regular customer, behaving normally and expecting fast and courteous service. Being too nice or too mean is a dead giveaway to an experienced teller.

Chapter Eight
Stock Certificates

Doing stock fraud is another relatively simple way of turning paper into money. There are several ways that this type of fraud can deliver a good return for the forger's investment of time and money. A discussion of two plans follows that will open one's eyes in this area. One plan has short-term requirements that will yield three or four times the forger's investment, depending upon the city he chooses to use and the number of banking systems it has. The second plan requires that the forger set up and maintain a more elaborate scam, but the return is substantial if he has the patience for it. Both of these operations will take an investment of the forger's time, as well as at least ten thousand dollars of start-up money. The first scam takes a week or two, while the second one requires at least six months to do properly, and it can last for years if the forger wants it to.

The first method is pretty straightforward, and the amount that the forger can make really depends upon the number of banks or finance companies that will make him a collateralized loan. The forger will need to establish a residence, so if he arranges to share a house or apartment with someone whom he contacts from a classified ad, for instance, it will be a lot easier than setting up his own place. The forger finds someone who works days, and by doing so ensures that the forger will be able to stay home during business hours and answer the phone calls from banks and loan companies. When anyone calls inquiring about the forger, he just assumes the role of the person they want to talk to: landlord, employer, reference, etc. The forger gives the inquirer information that corresponds with what he wrote on his loan applications. Who could do a better job of playing the pleased landlord, impressed employer, or well-connected business acquaintance that all creditors want their debtors to have? The loan-verification workers who make the calls are seldom the people who the forger was talking to in person, so voice recognition is usually not a problem. The forger needs to get a cellular telephone that he can always carry with him. The name he uses to initiate cellular phone service is unimportant, but he will need to have voice mail and messaging so that he can leave an answer message that implies a business where he is employed. Later in the scam, the forger will need the cell phone for a different application that I will explain. With these bases covered, the forger should be able to provide a residence and a place of employment for the banks and loan companies with which he will be doing business.

The forger's name will not be listed with the credit bureau(s) that the lending institutions check with, so he will need to come up with a believable story. For instance: he just arrived back in this country after an absence of at least five or six years. Mexico or Europe are good places to have been, but Canada is not. The forger must remember that his task is to be helpful, and since he is aware of his credit limitations, he will be glad to provide collateral for his loan in order to reestablish his credit and get his new life started. The forger wants to project the persona of an American citizen who was recently divorced from a person in Mexico or Europe or wherever, and has moved back to the good old USA to start over. If the forger offers the lending institutions stock as collateral, they will usually be glad to loan him about 75 or 80% of its face value. If the forger talks with banks and loan companies before he buys any stock, he can have all of his questions answered before he commits to anyone or anything connected to this crime. This is also a good way for the forger to determine just how much he stands to make on this scam, and if it's worth his time and trouble. Some locations are just too much trouble to do crimes in. I cannot explain why or how this happens; it just does. If the forger isn't happy with the way the situation is developing, he should move on to another place that feels right.

The forger will not have to provide the lending institutions with any stock information at the moment he talks to them. He just tells them the stock's approximate value and his immediate financial needs, so that they can calculate the loan information and tell the forger what it will take to make him the loan. Once the forger has taken care of all of the preliminaries and has a person to deal with, he can then get some stock and duplicate it as many times as it takes to satisfy all of his loan-requirement needs. The forger will be selling the original stock back to a brokerage when he is done with it, so he mustn't get it confused with the fake stuff. Stock is created and distributed from many locations, so nothing is ever identical, and the industry depends upon the numbers for verification of authenticity. If the forger settles for fabricating stock certificates that are 97% correct, he will be fine. By the time the loan officer has the forger's phony stock certificates on his desk, most of the paperwork will already be done. At this point, all the loan officer will do is call and verify the documents. He will do this in the forger's presence, since it would be wrong to ask him to surrender the certificates until the loan is made.

The certificates should never leave the forger's sight until he has the loan. They are not just worthless pieces of paper, and should be treated with respect. Since the forger purchased the initial stock legally, when the loan officer's call is made for verification, it will come back as OK. The lending institution has forms and procedures for notifying the Securities Exchange Commission (SEC) of the forger's loan, so the only information that the phone call will supply is that the stock is good. It does not matter how many lending institutions call to verify the stock; the only answer they will get is "yes" or "no" regarding its authenticity. The forger can tell any story he wants to about its origin, or his possession of it, since the time frame of one's ownership of stock is not public knowledge. Since the forger has requested a normal service from a lending institution, his loan will be just another day's work to a place that requires a steady supply of borrowers to remain in business. Once the loan is made to the forger, the certificates he gave the bank will be put into a file and forgotten until the borrower pays off the loan or defaults on it. If, at any time, the forger feels the need to postpone the discovery of his fake stock, he need only continue to make the loan payments. Stock certificates come in a variety of sizes and shapes, so the forger just buys several different sorts until he finds the one he can work with and reproduce well enough to use. The forger can always resell the ones he does not use to a brokerage later. This is really a lot simpler than it might sound, so the astute forger will not disregard this possibility too quickly.

The second method is more complicated, but as usual, that complication is the reason for its greater reward. This scam has the potential for millions, and I have seen it done to the tune of $25 million in Denver in 1986-87. The forgers did not have the technology that is around today, and they had to do it the hard way, but it was done successfully. The newspapers from that time will provide the story, if anyone is interested in a view from the outside. The inside view of this method is given here, to better explain how the forger does it on a smaller scale. There is virtually no way to prevent this type of setup, so its life span lasts until the forger runs out of sheep.

The objective of the forger in this instance is to acquire the education and information necessary to open his own brokerage in order to sell the phony certificates that he creates. This actually requires a lot less work than it sounds like it does, and the new stock buyers that are entering the market on a regular basis supply all of the customers the forger will ever need for this scam. The major difference with this plan is that the forger will be required to lie face-to-face to many people; you know, sort of like a priest or a politician.

If the forger looks in the want ads of most big newspapers, he will probably find an advertisement that reads along the lines of "Wanted, *Stock Broker Trainee*, no experience needed, will train on the job." These sorts of ads are always in the newspaper because the turnover rate is very high in this business. Most commercial brokerages are always looking for the ambitious few who will make a career out of this profession. The forger need only dress for the part, and he will probably be hired by the first brokerage to which he applies. The brokerage will spend a few weeks training the forger in the "how to's," and then he will be given a desk and a set of directions for locating new customers. The brokerage will show the forger how to sell stock and create new accounts for investing other people's money. As soon as he feels competent in this skill, the forger takes all of the information that he can with him and says his good-byes.

Most major newspapers carry advertisements for entry-level positions in securities and stock brokerages, and the forger sometimes makes use of these positions to learn the necessary skills for his endeavors.

The forger finds and rents an office that will allow him to duplicate the operation he just left. His ersatz brokerage won't be as large, but the concept will be the same. The forger won't be hiring anyone until he is up and running. He doesn't have to hire anyone at all if he wants to do it by himself. The whole operation is less complicated if the forger does it on his own, but after he has been at it for awhile his enhanced confidence will probably convince the forger to hire a couple of rookies to do the work for him. The idea is for the forger to do just what he did at the real brokerage; cold-call potential customers and sell them stock. Cold-calling is less complicated than dealing with established customers, because most new clients are not real familiar with the process. They will accept the forger's answers to any of the questions they might ask, and his inexperience will not be noticed. The process for finding new customers that the forger learned during his brokerage training will oftentimes surprise him with the results he gets. It's actually quite simple to sell this stuff, and the profits are pretty high, too.

The forger: "There's one born every minute..."
His prey: "We're gonna make a fortune! This guy really knows his stuff!"

Once the forger has convinced a customer to buy certain stocks from him, he then buys a share of that stock and duplicates it as many times as he needs to in order to fill that order. There are various other pieces of paper that the forger will need to create, but they are really just contracts and receipts, and are easy to fabricate compared to the other documents he will be forging. The forger's sales will be made over the phone, so he will have the time required for making the new stock certificates. The forger just tells the client that the stock certificates and documentation can be sent via a messenger service, or can be picked up in person by the client the next day. Either way, the forger is not expected to have the stock certificates just lying on his desk as soon as he makes arrangements to buy them from the exchange, so a delay is normal and expected.

While the forger is training at the brokerage, he steals one of their licenses from the wall and creates one for himself, along with a few diplomas that will look good on his wall as well. The more professional-looking the forger's office is, the more he will come across as a good investment to his clients. The forger should also request, in writing, a list of the licensed brokers in the state in which he's working. This list is commonly available in the industry, so the forger just asks someone while he's working at the brokerage. They might even have a list there somewhere that the forger can copy. The forger's plan is to locate several brokers that are in other cities, and use their ID numbers to do business when a number is required. Most of the transactions done in this business are done through messengers anyway, so the forger can always be pretend to be an employee of another brokerage when it suits the situation.

If the forger ever has a problem with a client concerning his stock or money, he offers to buy the client out on the spot with no loss to him for the trouble. Not only will the client not be able to find another deal like the one the forger is offering, but if he ever does decide to sell out, the forger will be his first choice, and that is what the forger wants anyway. It keeps the forger's business separate from the world outside, and it remains his secret. The forger lets it be known that his brokerage's reputation is to always offer its clients a better deal than any other firm will. By doing so, the forger is always aware of his clients' actions, and can make his getaway if need be. Word of mouth is a common method of getting business, so if the forger treats a dissatisfied customer with kindness and quick refunds, he will get customers from places he didn't even know existed. The forger must *always* remember that this is a game of illusion. He needs to play by the rules that allow him to win, or else not play at all.

The game plan is for the forger to sell phony stock until he has the amount of money he wants, and then split. It's a pretty simple concept, when one thinks about it. There is no need for the forger to complicate matters by worrying about things that he cannot control. The physical paperwork that the forger actually provides his clients just sits in filing cabinets anyway. There is no one to examine it and tell the client that it is fake, and it is not something that one shows to friends or carries around for the sake of bragging. I own plenty of legitimate stock, and I can't recall ever showing it to a single person for any reason. It's pretty much left alone once the initial transaction is complete. This is one crime in which the product is not handled by very many people, and the ones who do handle it are not experts in its manufacture. There are small variations in all printed documents; just look at money. Most people do not know enough about stock certificates to spot fraud, and would be embarrassed to show their ignorance anyway. If there is ever a major problem, the forger will be the first one asked to resolve it. His first indication will be a call from the SEC or one of its agents. The forger stalls the caller with a lie and packs his belongings. He might not have gotten what he wanted, but he got enough to know how to do it better the next time. The wily forger smiles, waves good-bye as he closes the door behind him, and doesn't look back.

Chapter Nine
Trust Deeds

Even the name of this document is cause for concern. When one considers that most of the people who deal in trust deeds are crooks themselves, the idea of defrauding them is almost funny. It's even funnier when one realizes that the ultimate goal is to trade a trust deed for the only other document in circulation that bears the word "trust" on it: the dollar bill. Both of these pieces of paper are used to represent the promise of something requiring trust on *your* part.

A trust deed is a piece of paper that represents entire or partial ownership in real property. Real property can be defined as dirt, with or without a structure on it. The concept represented here is that the forger will duplicate this simple document and sell or borrow against it. The process for verifying the authenticity or ownership of this sort of document is very easily defeated, and that makes it a prime target for crimes of fraud.

Deeds are bought and sold by the tens of thousands every business day in this country, It has become such a common transaction that the process has been reduced to a task of extreme simplicity. If verification of ownership is desired, a phone call or a visit to the local county courthouse is all that is needed. He makes a note of the address he is interested in, as well as another one that is close by. The forger then either goes to the country recorder at the courthouse himself, or obtains the services of a service which handles such chores (using a false name, of course). By asking for information on the nearby address, the forger eliminates any record of his search for the address in which he is really interested. They will all be on the same piece of microfiche, which are small sheets of film on which many pages of microcopied information are recorded. The information under discussion is recorded according to address. So, since there are multiple addresses on each sheet of film, the forger (or the service he employs) leaves no record of requesting any information for that particular address, and thus reduces the potential number of people who might recognize or remember him later, when they are questioned by the authorities. All that the forger or the service has to do is request an address from the country recorder, and the film with that information on it is made available. These are public records, so there is no fuss (or even ID) required to see them. If the forger or the service wants copies of any of these documents, he just asks and they are provided to him for a small charge.

In this scam the forger can only double or triple his investment, but since there is little risk of losing his investment, the amount he puts up should be substantial. The basic concept here is to purchase a valid deed with a fair-to-middling market value, and then to resell it to as many different buyers simultaneously as the forger can line up. He will resell it with a loss of 5 to 10%, but that is the profit margin the buyers are looking for, so it is negotiable.

The forger looks in the newspaper's classified ads and finds a deed that fits his needs, and then buys it and records it at the courthouse. He then places a classified ad offering to sell it, and makes calls to people who advertise that they buy deeds. It is pretty commonplace for people who just acquired a property to try and resell it. Lots of people invest in real estate and then find themselves in a situation that requires quick cash. If they have to take a loss to raise the needed money, then so be it. They can always write off the loss on their income tax returns, so it really isn't a loss to smart businessmen. It's just a business deal and nothing more. The newspaper's classified ads are full of people who are looking for deeds to buy. The forger calls up some of them and asks all of the questions that he wants answered in order to make himself comfortable in doing this scam. When the forger has the information that he needs, he starts trying to sell his deed. It's OK to have as many buyers ready to buy the forger's deeds as he can line up; it's no different than selling anything else. Dates are very important in tax strategies and divorce settlements, so the forger's need for a certain date and time frame for the close of escrow is commonplace and will raise no eyebrows. The forger makes duplicates of his paperwork, and has his appointments set up accordingly, so that they all go down on the same day, one-two-three.

Since the forger will most likely be getting paid with checks, he will have to have already set up accounts to deposit them. If possible, the forger asks that the buyer leave the *Pay To The Order* portion of the check blank; this is not an unusual request. There are often agents and people selling property for others, so leaving part of the check blank is not unheard of, and the forger needs to try hard to get his buyers to accommodate this request. This allows the forger to take the check to a local coin or gold shop and convert it to something he can use. The checks the forger gets will be large ones, and the banking system in this country makes getting sizable amounts of cash out at one time very difficult and often impossible. If the forger is forced to accept checks which are made out to him, then he just goes to his bank and has them exchanged for money orders that he can exchange for something else of value. The forger only has a short time to convert these checks, so he must plan his moves accordingly. If the forger does plan on converting his checks to gold, he should make arrangements a day or two ahead of time with several gold suppliers to assure that they can do it when he wants to. These places will sell the forger all of the gold he wishes to buy, regardless of the amount, but they need advance notice to do it. They will call the bank or take the check there to verify its validity, so the forger should expect them to do it, but since the check is real, it is no problem. The possibility does exist that the forger can just endorse the check that is made out to him over to the gold dealer. It is no big deal, really, and if the forger just plans his actions thoughtfully, everything will work out.

Document Fraud And Other Crimes Of Deception

58

AFTER RECORDING MAIL TO

Name _____

Address _____

City, State, Zip _____

Filed for Record at Request of

DEED OF TRUST
(For use in the state of Washington only)

THIS DEED OF TRUST, made this   day of   , 19   , between
, GRANTOR,

whose address is

, TRUSTEE,

whose address is   , and
, BENEFICIARY,

whose address is

WITNESSETH: Grantor hereby bargains, sells, and conveys to Trustee in trust, with power of sale, the following described real property in   County, Washington:

Assessor's Property Tax Parcel/Account Number:

which real property is not used principally for agricultural or farming purposes, together with all the tenements, hereditaments, and appurtenances now or hereafter thereunto belonging or in any wise appertaining, and the rents, issues, and profits thereof.

This deed is for the purpose of securing performance of each agreement of Grantor herein contained, and payment of the sum of _____ Dollars ($) with interest, in accordance with the terms of a promissory note of even date herewith, payable to Beneficiary or order, and made by Grantor, and all renewals, modifications, and extensions thereof, and also such further sums as may be advanced or loaned by Beneficiary to Grantor, or any of their successors or assigns, together with interest thereon at such rate as shall be agreed upon.

To protect the security of this Deed of Trust, Grantor covenants and agrees:

1. To keep the property in good condition and repair; to permit no waste thereof; to complete any building, structure, or improvement being built or about to be built thereon; to restore promptly any building, structure, or improvement thereon which may be damaged or destroyed; and to comply with all laws, ordinances, regulations, covenants, conditions, and restrictions affecting the property.

2. To pay before delinquent all lawful taxes and assessments upon the property; to keep the property free and clear of all other charges, liens, or encumbrances impairing the security of this Deed of Trust.

3. To keep all buildings now or hereafter erected on the property described herein continuously insured against loss by fire or other hazards in an amount not less than the total debt secured by this Deed of Trust. All policies shall be held by the Beneficiary, and be in such companies as the Beneficiary may approve and have loss payable first to the Beneficiary, as its interest may appear, and then to the Grantor. The amount collected under any insurance policy may be applied upon any indebtedness hereby secured in such order as the Beneficiary shall determine. Such application by the Beneficiary shall not cause discontinuance of any proceedings to foreclose this Deed of Trust. In the event of foreclosure, all rights of the Grantor in insurance policies then in force shall pass to the purchaser at the foreclosure sale.

4. To defend any action or proceeding purporting to affect the security hereof or the rights or powers of Beneficiary or Trustee, and to pay all costs and expenses, including cost of title search and attorney's fees in a reasonable amount, in any such action or proceeding, and in any suit brought by Beneficiary to foreclose this Deed of Trust.

*Trust deeds vary from state to state. An example of
Washington State trust deed is shown on this and the following page.*

5 To pay all costs, fees, and expenses in connection with this Deed of Trust, including the expenses of the Trustee incurred in enforcing the obligation secured hereby and Trustee's and attorney's fees actually incurred, as provided by statute

6 Should Grantor fail to pay when due any taxes, assessments, insurance premiums, liens, encumbrances, or other charges against the property hereinabove described, Beneficiary may pay the same, and the amount so paid, with interest at the rate set forth in the note secured hereby, shall be added to and become a part of the debt secured in this Deed of Trust

IT IS MUTUALLY AGREED THAT

1 In the event any portion of the property is taken or damaged in an eminent domain proceeding, the entire amount of the award or such portion as may be necessary to fully satisfy the obligation secured hereby, shall be paid to Beneficiary to be applied to said obligation

2 By accepting payment of any sum secured hereby after its due date, Beneficiary does not waive its right to require prompt payment when due of all other sums so secured or to declare default for failure to so pay

3 The Trustee shall reconvey all or any part of the property covered by this Deed of Trust to the person entitled thereto, on written request of the Grantor and the Beneficiary, or upon satisfaction of the obligation secured and written request for reconveyance made by the Beneficiary or the person entitled thereto

4 Upon default by Grantor in the payment of any indebtedness secured hereby or in the performance of any agreement contained herein, all sums secured hereby shall immediately become due and payable at the option of the Beneficiary. In such event and upon written request of Beneficiary, Trustee shall sell the trust property, in accordance with the Deed of Trust Act of the State of Washington, at public auction to the highest bidder. Any person except Trustee may bid at Trustee's sale. Trustee shall apply the proceeds of the sale as follows (1) to the expense of the sale, including a reasonable Trustee's fee and attorney's fee, (2) to the obligation secured by this Deed of Trust, and (3) the surplus, if any, shall be distributed to the persons entitled thereto

5 Trustee shall deliver to the purchaser at the sale its deed, without warranty, which shall convey to the purchaser the interest in the property which Grantor had or had the power to convey at the time of his execution of this Deed of Trust, and such as he may have acquired thereafter Trustee's deed shall recite the facts showing that the sale was conducted in compliance with all the requirements of law and of this Deed of Trust, which recital shall be prima facie evidence of such compliance and conclusive evidence thereof in favor of bona fide purchaser and encumbrancers for value

6 The power of sale conferred by this Deed of Trust and by the Deed of Trust Act of the State of Washington is not an exclusive remedy; Beneficiary may cause this Deed of Trust to be foreclosed as a mortgage

7 In the event of the death, incapacity, disability, or resignation of Trustee, Beneficiary may appoint in writing a successor trustee, and upon the recording of such appointment in the mortgage records of the county in which this Deed of Trust is recorded, the successor trustee shall be vested with all powers of the original trustee The trustee is not obligated to notify any party hereto of pending sale under any other Deed of Trust or of an action or proceeding in which Grantor, Trustee, or Beneficiary shall be a party unless such action or proceeding is brought by the Trustee

8 This Deed of Trust applies to, inures to the benefit of, and is binding not only on the parties hereto, but on their heirs, devisees, legatees, administrators, executors, and assigns The term Beneficiary shall mean the holder and owner of the note secured hereby, whether or not named as Beneficiary herein

STATE OF _____
COUNTY OF _____ } ss

I certify that I know or have satisfactory evidence that _____
_____ the person _____ who appeared before me, and said person _____ acknowledged that _____ signed this instrument and acknowledged it to be _____ free and voluntary act for the uses and purposes mentioned in this instrument

Dated _____

Notary Public in and for the State of _____
Residing at _____
My appointment expires: _____

REQUEST FOR FULL RECONVEYANCE - *Do not record To be used only when note has been paid*
TO TRUSTEE

The undersigned is the legal owner and holder of the note and all other indebtedness secured by the within Deed of Trust Said note, together with all other indebtedness secured by said Deed of Trust, has been fully paid and satisfied, and you are hereby requested and directed, on payment to you of any sums owing to you under the terms of said Deed of Trust, to cancel said note above mentioned, and all other evidences of indebtedness secured by said Deed of Trust delivered to you herewith, together with the said Deed of Trust, and to reconvey, without warranty, to the parties designated by the terms of said Deed of Trust, all the estate now held by you thereunder

Dated _____, 19 _____

60

The forger can also borrow money against the property from several banks at the same time, if he sets it up so that all of the loans happen on the same day. He can also borrow money against the property and sell it to another person or two at the same time. The options are many; the forger is the one doing this, so it's strictly his call. The forger figures that the paperwork involved with what he is selling to people is a relatively slow process, and 24 to 48 hours is a good time frame to work with. The forger is not breaking any laws until he actually sells the deed to more than one person or bank, so he should get comfortable with his game plan before he makes his move.

The forger need merely look through the newspaper to find numerous advertisements placed by those who offer to pay quick cash for trust deeds, mortgages, contracts, and other negotiable instruments.

As a second twist to this type of plan, the forger can assume the identity of a person who has equity in a property, and then sell or borrow against that equity just as in the above-mentioned scam. All of the information that the forger needs in order to do this is available at the courthouse in the paperwork for the property he is scamming. The person whose identity the forger is assuming might also have other property recorded there, and this can provide the forger with lucrative information. The forger can find a property that suits him by looking at some of the files from a good neighborhood. When he finds a property that he likes, the forger just files a notarized (by him) second or third deed of trust at the courthouse and he is in business. There is no mechanism of notification to the owners of the property on which the forger files the second or third deed of trust. He must make sure that when he provides the county with an address at which he will receive future paperwork concerning the property, that it is not the same address as the property itself, and then the forger will have covered all of the bases that *might* hurt him. The actual owner will most likely never know that the second or third deed of trust has been filed, until they are eventually notified by the person who lent the forger money. If the forger tells the lender that the property is a rental, the lender will not bother to notify the people living there of what is going on. There are literally hundreds of potential lenders of money in every city, and they exchange little, if any, information between themselves. If the forger never discusses any other business with the people he meets, they will never know that he is doing business with someone else, and the forger will run little risk of crossing himself up. This is not a difficult crime, but it is a professional one, and if the forger treats it as such, he can make out very well for his time and trouble.

Chapter Ten
Quitclaim Deed Fraud
in a Nutshell

QUITCLAIM DEED: A document by which a person releases or relinquishes any or all claim or interest or title to some form of property or right without guaranteeing or warranting the validity of such title.

In English, a quitclaim deed is a fast and commonly used method of selling or borrowing against a property, whether that property is developed or not. Although it is often easier for the forger to select and use an undeveloped piece of real estate, the more skillful forger often uses *income property*, since such properties are often very plentiful and have the added advantage of having a cash flow that will allow for a larger group of potential lenders. Either method is lucrative and not very difficult, so I will address the basic steps that work for both, and add the few additional steps required for income property at the end.

The first step is to acquire a quitclaim deed, and this can be done by visiting almost any well-stocked office-supply store in any city in the country. The deeds are generic, so where they are acquired is not important. But since a property's value is determined by an appraisal, the forger needs to get some appraisal forms at the same time he picks up the quitclaim deed forms.

64

QUITCLAIM DEED

THIS QUITCLAIM DEED, Executed this   day of   , 19

by first party,

whose post office address is

to second party,

whose post office address is

   WITNESSETH, That the said first party, for good consideration and for the sum of
                Dollars ($) paid by the said second party, the receipt whereof is hereby
acknowledged, does hereby remise, release and quitclaim unto the said second party forever, all the right, title, interest and claim which the said first party has in and to the following described parcel of land, and improvements and
appurtenances thereto in the County of   , State of   to wit:

   IN WITNESS WHEREOF, The said first party has signed and sealed these presents the day and year first
above written. Signed, sealed and delivered in presence of:

_____   _____
Signature of Witness   Signature of First Party

_____   _____
Print name of Witness   Print name of First Party

_____   _____
Signature of Witness   Signature of First Party

_____   _____
Print name of Witness   Print name of First Party

State of   }
County of
On   before me,
appeared   ,
personally known to me (or proved to me on the basis of satisfactory evidence) to be the person(s) whose name(s)
is/are subscribed to the within instrument and acknowledged to me that he/she/they executed the same in his/her/their
authorized capacity(ies), and that by his/her/their signature(s) on the instrument the person(s), or the entity upon
behalf of which the person(s) acted, executed the instrument.
WITNESS my hand and official seal.

_____
Signature of Notary   Affiant _____Known_____Produced ID
                                                        Type of ID _____
                              APHT   (Seal)
                                                                    (Revised 12/95)

*There are many form of quitclaim deeds. Two are depicted on this and
the following page.*

THIS INDENTURE, made the _____ day of _____,
19_____

BETWEEN (the name and address of the person executing the
deed), party of the first part, and (name and address of the person to
whom it is given), party of the second part,

WITNESSETH, that the party of the first part, in consideration of
(indicate the amount) dollars, lawful money of the United States paid
by the party of the second part, does hereby remise, release and
quitclaim unto the party of the second part, his heirs and assigns
forever, ALL (here the actual interest of the party executing the
quitclaim deed is to be stated and the land described relating to
which this interest exists)

TOGETHER with all right, title and interest, if any, of the party of the
first part in and to any streets and roads abutting the above
described premises to the center lines thereof.

TOGETHER with the appurtenances and all the estate and rights of
the party of the first part in and to said premises.

TO HAVE AND TO HOLD the premises herein granted unto the party
of the second part and his assigns forever.

IN WITNESS WHEREOF, the party of the first part has executed this
deed the day and year first above written.

In presence of: (Signature of grantor)

Witness
                         ACKNOWLEDGMENT

Next, the forger needs to find a suitable property, and since there
is always a chance of failure for some unforeseen reason, the
skillful forger often does this scam on multiple properties, using
different false identities on each so that even with a high failure rate
there is a real good chance of success on at least one of the
properties. If all of the properties pan out, then the forger needs to
set the closing dates on the loans or sales of the properties for the
same day, so that all of the business can be accomplished in as
short a time frame as possible. This provides an opportunity for a
clean escape before someone files the new deeds, and the action on
the property falls under scrutiny by the courthouse staff, whose job

is keeping monthly track of high-ticket real estate transactions for a myriad of bureaucratic reasons that have no relevance here.

Once the forger finds the desired property, he notes the address and one nearby (as explained in the chapter on trust deed fraud), and either he or a service he employs goes to the courthouse and requests the information on the nearby property by merely asking a clerk whose job it is to supply such public information to all who ask for it.

When the forger has found the right set of circumstances on a particular property, such as a low to non-existing debt, and/or an owner who lives out of town or state, he simply writes down all of the information, and makes a reasonable facsimile of the owner's signature as a reference. Since the false signature will eventually be discovered, it is not necessary to reproduce it perfectly. It is becoming more and more common for one's identification to be requested when asking for property information from the courthouse. By not specifying the property, and not asking for any photocopies of the documents but instead jotting down the pertinent information, the forger reduces his risk of exposure even further. Many courthouses have some sort of video surveillance to document events that might be needed at a later date, and these devices register time and date, so the professional forger does nothing that will identify him to the camera, such as asking for a particular address or copies of information pertaining to a particular address. There are crime task forces (especially in larger cities) which have the specific mission of investigating document-fraud crimes, and they are frequently very good at their job and know all of the tricks, such as checking the tapes for obvious and often-overlooked mistakes which are made by foolish or careless forgers.

All of the information that is needed to falsify a quitclaim deed can be written down, so there is no need for the astute forger to ever be remembered if he is careful in his actions. The professional forger knows that he can begin his search dozens of addresses away from the actual address he desires to learn about, and that by asking for copies of different addresses on the same segment of microfiche film, he can further reduce his risk.

Once all of the needed information is acquired, the forger need only fill in the blank quitclaim deed, using information that corresponds to his false identity, and have the document notarized. A phony notary seal is no problem for the forger, and since the notary seal is an accepted form of authenticity, the forger always uses it, even in states which do not require it. The appearance of a notary seal has a way of reducing stress or anxiety on the potential lender's part, and is the mark of a true professional.

The forger will also fill in the information on a blank appraisal form by taking the name and amounts from the microfiche and using the actual appraisal company's name. Thus, when a potential lender is checking the information for accuracy, the company that did the appraisal will verify the forger's appraisal over the phone, and the matter will end there. The potential lender will not need to request a copy of the appraisal that will have the owner's *real* signature on it instead of the forger's version that the potential lender has in the loan package.

The concept here is to eliminate all of the original owner's signatures and replace them with the forger's versions, so that everything looks the same on all of the necessary paperwork. By the time money changes hands, there will be at least three or more documents that will bear the forger's version of the owner's signature, so they all need to be taken into consideration and replaced if possible. The good news for the forger is that they are actually easily replaced.

Once all of the paperwork is complete, the forger then goes to the courthouse and records his new quitclaim deed. For all intents and purposes, the forger now owns the property. Once the deed is recorded, the forger can do all of the things a real owner can do with the property, such as sell it or borrow against its equity.

68

COMPLETE SUMMARY REPORT
UNIFORM RESIDENTIAL APPRAISAL REPORT   File No. _____

Property Description

| Property Address | | | City | | | State | Zip Code |

Legal Description

County

Assessor's Parcel No _____   Tax Year _____   R.E. Taxes $ _____   Special Assessments $ _____

Borrower _____   Current Owner _____   Occupant ☐ Owner ☐ Tenant ☐ Vacant

Property rights appraised ☐ Fee Simple ☐ Leasehold   Project Type ☐ PUD ☐ Condominium (HUD/VA only)   HOA$ _____ /Mo

Neighborhood/Project Name _____   Map Reference _____   Census Tract _____

Sale Price $ _____   Date of Sale _____   Description and $ amount of loan charges/concessions to be paid by seller

Lender/Client _____   Address _____

Appraiser _____   Address _____

Location	☐ Urban	☐ Suburban	☐ Rural	**Predominant occupancy**	**Single family housing** PRICE $(000) / AGE (yrs)	**Present land use %**	**Land use change**
Built up	☐ Over 75%	☐ 25-75%	☐ Under 25%			One family _____	☐ Not likely ☐ Likely
Growth rate	☐ Rapid	☐ Stable	☐ Slow	☐ Owner	Low	2-4 family _____	☐ In process
Property values	☐ Increasing	☐ Stable	☐ Declining	☐ Tenant	High	Multi-family _____	To _____
Demand/supply	☐ Shortage	☐ In balance	☐ Over supply	☐ Vacant (0-5%)	Predominant	Commercial _____	
Marketing time	☐ Under 3 mos	☐ 3-6 mos.	☐ Over 6 mos.	☐ Vacant (over 5%)		( )	

Note: Race and the racial composition of the neighborhood are not appraisal factors.

Neighborhood boundaries & characteristics _____

Factors that affect the marketability of the properties in the neighborhood (proximity to employment and amenities, employment stability, appeal to market, etc.)

Market conditions in the subject neighborhood (including support for the above conclusions related to the trend of property values, demand/supply, and marketing time — — such as data on competitive properties for sale in the neighborhood, description of the prevalence of sales and financing concessions, etc.)

PUD

Project information for PUDs (if applicable) – – Is the developer/builder in control of the Home Owners' Association (HOA)? ☐ Yes ☐ No

Approximate total number of units in the subject project _____   Approximate total number of units for sale in the subject project _____

Describe common elements and recreational facilities _____

SITE

Dimensions _____	Topography _____
Site area _____ Corner Lot ☐ Yes ☐ No	Size _____
Specific zoning classification and description _____	Shape _____
Zoning compliance ☐ Legal ☐ Legal nonconforming (Grandfathered use) ☐ Illegal ☐ No Zoning	Drainage _____
Highest & best use as improved: ☐ Present use ☐ Other use (explain)	View _____

Utilities	Public	Other	Off-site improvements	Type	Public	Private	Landscaping _____
Electricity	☐	_____	Street	_____	☐	☐	Driveway Surface _____
Gas	☐	_____	Curb/gutter	_____	☐	☐	Apparent easements _____
Water	☐	_____	Sidewalk	_____	☐	☐	FEMA Special Flood Hazard Area ☐ Yes ☐ No
Sanitary sewer	☐	_____	Street lights	_____	☐	☐	FEMA Zone _____ Map Date _____
Storm Sewer	☐	_____	Alley	_____	☐	☐	FEMA Map No. _____

Comments (apparent adverse easements, encroachments, special assessments, slide areas, illegal or legal nonconforming zoning, use, etc.) _____

IMPROVEMENTS

GENERAL DESCRIPTION	EXTERIOR DESCRIPTION	FOUNDATION	BASEMENT	INSULATION
No. of Units _____	Foundation _____	Slab _____	Area Sq. Ft. _____	Roof _____ ☐
No. of Stories _____	Exterior Walls _____	Crawl Space _____	% Finished _____	Ceiling _____ ☐
Type (Det./Att.) _____	Roof Surface _____	Basement _____	Ceiling _____	Walls _____ ☐
Design (Style) _____	Gutters & Dwnspts _____	Sump Pump _____	Walls _____	Floor _____ ☐
Existing/Proposed _____	Window Type _____	Dampness _____	Floor _____	None _____ ☐
Age (Yrs.) _____	Storm/Screens _____	Settlement _____	Outside Entry _____	Unknown _____ ☐
Effective Age (Yrs.) _____	Manufactured House _____	Infestation _____		

ROOM LIST

ROOMS	Foyer	Living	Dining	Kitchen	Den	Family Rm.	Rec. Rm.	Bedrooms	# Baths	Laundry	Other	Area Sq. Ft.
Basement												
Level 1												
Level 2												

Finished area above grade contains: _____ Rooms; _____ Bedroom(s); _____ Bath(s); _____ Square Feet of Gross Living Area

DESCRIPTION

INTERIOR	Materials/Condition	HEATING		KITCHEN EQUIP	ATTIC		AMENITIES		CAR STORAGE	
Floors	_____	Type _____		Refrigerator ☐	None	☐	Fireplace(s)# _____		None ☐	
Walls	_____	Fuel _____		Range/Oven ☐	Stairs	☐	Patio _____		Garage _____ # of cars	
Trim/Finish	_____	Condition _____		Disposal ☐	Drop Stair	☐	Deck _____		Attached _____	
Bath Floor	_____	COOLING		Dishwasher ☐	Scuttle	☐	Porch _____		Detached _____	
Bath Wainscot	_____	Central _____		Fan/Hood ☐	Floor	☐	Fence _____		Built-in _____	
Doors	_____	Other _____		Microwave ☐	Heated	☐	Pool _____		Carport _____	
		Condition _____		Washer/Dryer ☐	Finished	☐			Driveway _____	

Additional features (special energy efficient items, etc.) _____

COMMENTS

Condition of the improvements, depreciation (physical, functional, and external), repairs needed, quality of construction, remodeling/additions, etc. _____

Adverse environmental conditions (such as, but not limited to, hazardous wastes, toxic substances, etc.) present in the improvements, on the site, or in the immediate vicinity of the subject property _____

Appraisal forms vary, but this and the following page
depict a commonly used version

| Valuation Section | UNIFORM RESIDENTIAL APPRAISAL REPORT | File No. |

COST APPROACH

ESTIMATED SITE VALUE	= $	Comments on Cost Approach (such as source of cost estimate,
ESTIMATED REPRODUCTION COST-NEW-OF IMPROVEMENTS		site value, square foot calculation and, for HUD, VA, and FmHA, the
Dwelling _____ Sq Ft @ $ _____ = $ _____		estimated remaining economic life of the property)
_____ Sq Ft @ $ _____ = _____		
Garage/Carport _____ Sq Ft @ $ _____ = _____		
Total Estimated Cost New	= $	
Less Physical	Functional	External		
Depreciation	= $	
Depreciated Value of Improvements	= $	
"As-is" Value of Site Improvements	= $	
INDICATED VALUE BY COST APPROACH	= $	

SALES COMPARISON ANALYSIS

ITEM	SUBJECT	COMPARABLE NO. 1	COMPARABLE NO. 2	COMPARABLE NO. 3
Address				
Proximity to Subject				
Sales Price	$	$	$	$
Price/Gross Liv. Area	$	$	$	$
Data and/or Verification Sources				

VALUE ADJUSTMENTS	DESCRIPTION	DESCRIPTION	+(-)$Adjustment	DESCRIPTION	+(-)$Adjustment	DESCRIPTION	+(-)$Adjustment
Sales or Financing Concessions							
Date of Sale/Time							
Location							
Leasehold/Fee Simple							
Site							
View							
Design and Appeal							
Quality of Construction							
Age							
Condition							
Above Grade Room Count	Total	Bdrms	Baths	Total	Bdrms	Baths	Total	Bdrms	Baths	Total	Bdrms	Baths
Gross Living Area	Sq Ft	Sq Ft	Sq Ft	Sq Ft
Basement & Finished Rooms Below Grade							
Functional Utility							
Heating/Cooling							
Energy Efficient Items							
Garage/Carport							
Porch, Patio, Deck, Fireplace(s), etc							
Fence, Pool, etc							
Net Adj. (total)		+	-	$	+	-	$	+	-	$
Adjusted Sales Price of Comparable		% Net % Grs. $	% Net % Grs. $	% Net % Grs. $

Comments on Sales Comparison (including the subject property's compatibility to the neighborhood, etc.)

ITEM	SUBJECT	COMPARABLE NO. 1	COMPARABLE NO. 2	COMPARABLE NO. 3
Date, Price and Data Source for prior sales within year of appraisal				

Analysis of any current agreement of sale, option, or listing of the subject property and analysis of any prior sales of subject and comparables within one year of the date of appraisal

INDICATED VALUE BY SALES COMPARISON APPROACH		$
INDICATED VALUE BY INCOME APPROACH (if Applicable) Estimated Market Rent $ _____ /Mo. X Gross Rent Multiplier _____		= $

This appraisal is made [ ] "as is" [ ] subject to the repairs, alterations, inspections, or conditions listed below [ ] subject to completion per plans and specifications.

Conditions of Appraisal:

Final Reconciliation:

RECONCILIATION

The purpose of this appraisal is to estimate the market value of the real property that is the subject of this report, based on the above conditions and the certification, contingent and limiting conditions, and market value definition that are stated in the attached Freddie Mac Form 439/Fannie Mae Form 1004B (Revised _____).

I (WE) ESTIMATE THE MARKET VALUE, AS DEFINED, OF THE REAL PROPERTY THAT IS THE SUBJECT OF THIS REPORT, AS OF _____ (WHICH IS THE DATE OF INSPECTION AND THE EFFECTIVE DATE OF THIS REPORT) TO BE $ _____

APPRAISER	SUPERVISORY APPRAISER (ONLY IF REQUIRED):	
Signature	Signature	[ ] Did [ ] Did Not Inspect Property
Name	Name	
Date Report Signed	Date Report Signed	
State Certification # _____ State	State Certification # _____ State	
Or State License # _____ State	Or State License # _____ State	

As there is a growing awareness of this type of scam, the adept forger knows that to ensure that there is no special service offered by the county, such as notification to the owner of any and all action taken in regards to his or her property, he merely asks the clerk if such services are available, as if he is interested in taking advantage of it to protect his own property. He will then know if he needs to take precautions to make certain that this process is circumvented before initiating his scam. To bypass or beat this new and poorly handled notification system, the professional forger simply calls the courthouse and has a clerk change the notification address and/or telephone number in their records, as if the real owner has changed residency or telephone service. When the forger begins his scam, the mailing or phone call from the courthouse will go to the destination specified by the forger. Not all counties offer this service, but the forger covers his ass by requesting this service whether it is in place or not, and thus further reduces his liability factor by a notch. Some counties simply place a written notice in the owner's file that will not be discovered until it is too late for the forger to stop the wheels that he has set in motion, so this is an important precaution for the 21st-century forger to consider.

Many potential lenders will require a walk-through of the property they are considering accepting as equity for a loan, so if it is an income property, the forger will act like a potential lender and make a walk-through himself, just to see how the tenants will respond to a potential lender's appearance at their door asking for a look inside. If there is a problem, then the forger has time to either abort the scam at that address or do the walk-through with a potential lender at a time when he knows that the problem will not arise. The lender is at the mercy of the owner in this business, because he needs to make secured loans in order to generate profits and stay in business. The forger realizes this, and uses this knowledge to manipulate the lender into doing things the way the forger wants them done. He sets times and conditions that the lender must adhere to if he wishes to please the forger and make the loan.

Many tenants do not like any type of intrusion, and telling a potential lender that a walk-through is not possible is not only common, but easily accepted, as long as the rent roll records and appraisal are already provided. And in many cases the rent roll records are not required, because the owner does not wish to make them available to anyone, and the loan is based solely upon the value of the property. But the lender knows that there is an income on the property, and that has a positive bearing, whether the actual amount is disclosed or not. Lenders will always expect to see some form of the property, be it a photograph, drive-by, or walk-through. If the property is undeveloped land, a photograph of the surrounding properties is always a big plus for the forger, because it shows the potential lender the condition of the neighboring properties and often replaces the lender's doing anything else besides looking at the photographs. The forger will have a number of photographs taken from the property at different angles, just as a form of professionalism, as well as a courtesy which makes the potential lender's decision easier and quicker.

The forger can readily make himself aware of the current trends and nuances of the ever-changing real estate business by merely acting like a real buyer of a similar property, and having several sellers or lenders give him a list of the required documentation which is needed to secure the property. This is an easy way for the forger to acquire a list to work from. The information is there if it is sought correctly.

Chapter Eleven
Vehicle Titles

Duplicating and passing automobile titles is not only very easy, but it offers a good return on the forger's investment of time and money. The forger should have the equipment and the knowledge to use it by this stage of the game, so he will move on to the actual acquisition of vehicles to sell or borrow against. The idea is for the forger to have the vehicles in his possession legally, so that he can show them to any potential buyers or bankers whom he intends to do business with. The forger cannot go out and hot-wire a few vehicles to use, or buy stolen ones. Those methods are a dead end, and should never be considered as an option. Getting good, clean, *legal* vehicles to work with is really quite easy if the forger uses his head and employs a few well-placed lies.

The best method of obtaining the vehicles the forger needs is to rent them from one of the big automobile-rental agencies. They have the best new, low-mileage, fully loaded cars and vans around, and the forger gets to pick the ones he wants... what could be sweeter than that? The forger will need a credit card to facilitate the rental process, and several cards will make it even easier. If the forger does not have a credit card that he can use and then lose, he uses the methods described in the bonded credit card section of this book (Chapter 12). The forger will also have to use and lose at least one set of ID, and possibly several, depending upon the extent of his caper. ID and credit cards are used in almost all types of work, so the forger must become familiar with their acquisition.

The forger's first step is to obtain and duplicate some titles. The master title needs to be new and wrinkle-free. The forger can apply to any state for a new one to work with. All he needs is a paid-for vehicle, and it doesn't have to be new or even in the forger's name. The forger will need the title for only a few minutes, and information such as the name and address of the real owner will be changed once he has it stored in his computer, so the title's origin is unimportant and will not be revealed. Each state has its own version of this document, so the forger can use any one he wants to, and should probably use several in his endeavors. Once the forger has a title to use, he scans it into his system and removes all of the unwanted information, such as all of the information on the title that is not printed by the state. If the forger starts with a blank title, all of the information that he types or signs on the new one will look original. The forger will match the paper and print a batch of blank titles for himself. He doesn't have to be exact on the paper match, but he should get as close as possible. Regular toner is fine for car titles, and a notary stamp from the same state as that which issued the original title is also needed.

The forger is ready to get started. He takes his credit card to the airport and rents himself a car or van. The forger tells the rental person that he would like to pay cash when he returns the vehicle, so he would appreciate it if they would wait until he returns the car to collect the rental fee. The rental agency will still run a verification check on the forger's credit card, but they won't reduce his credit limit on it, and that will allow the forger to use it over and over again, even with a relatively low credit limit. Lots of people ask for just such a courtesy, and most rental agencies will be glad to do this. The forger rents the vehicle on a weekly basis, because this will give him plenty of time to do his thing and not have vehicles that have been reported stolen parked nearby.

*The forger can find a multiplicity of vehicle
rental outlets at any major airport.*

The forger drives the vehicle to another city and state and parks it at a place that he can work out of safely. Any other city and state will do, as long as it also has a big airport. The forger leaves the vehicle at the place to which he drove it, and goes to the airport to rent another new vehicle from another rental agency. He drives the second car back to the city where he started, and parks it at another secure place. The forger knows that there is no heat on him or his actions, so he takes his time and does it right. He goes back to the first airport and rents another vehicle from a third rental agency and drives it back to the second city. The forger repeats this procedure until he has all of the cars he wants to work with. He can use the same rental agency if he wishes, as there is no reason to deny him a second vehicle if he desires to rent one. These vehicles are worth fifteen to twenty thousand dollars each, and the forger's return will be 75% of that amount, so he doesn't sweat the outlay of cash to set this up. It will cost the forger a couple of hundred dollars per vehicle before he is done, but he already knows the expected return, so laying out the money is not stressful.

The forger sometimes visits an automobile dealership in order to purloin a sales contract book.

The reason that the forger went to different cities to obtain the vehicles is simply a precaution, but if he can add some confusion to the other team's anticipated pursuit, then he does so. The vehicles the forger will be getting from the different states will be recorded in those states' respective Department of Motor Vehicles computers, so by taking the vehicles to a second state the forger can avoid a hassle when it comes time to register the vehicles in the name he is using. Most automobile rental agencies register their vehicles locally, so the forger just checks each vehicle's license plate, and knows for sure if he has succeeded in his goal. The forger is not going to be selling the cars as if they are stolen, so not only does he make more money per vehicle, but he does not have to act like a crook or do business with any. This method takes a little time, but the results are worth it, and it's virtually trouble-free. One of the major pluses of dealing with cars which are stolen by this method is that the forger is never driving a reportedly stolen car, and he will always have either the rental paperwork or the legally issued registration with him. The savvy forger doesn't confuse this type of work with boosting cars or joy-riding. This is by no means small-time crime, and if caught in this act, he will be dealt with accordingly.

Continuing onward, the forger goes to several automobile dealerships around any city and gets himself some sales contract books that car lots always have just scattered about in those little offices that they have. If the forger goes to several dealerships, the chance to pick one up will eventually present itself. The forger asks a salesman to let him make a telephone call to find out when his wife will be getting to the dealership. This is a common sort of request, and it puts the forger into a room with a desk and, most likely, some of the contract books. If the forger carries a briefcase or some such contrivance into which to put the purloined contract books, the petty theft will be easier. The forger might want to acquire these contract books before he rents the vehicles, since they are pretty universal except for the dealership's name on the top. The forger can use any of them for any of the cars, regardless of the car's make. If the forger cannot get the contract books from a dealership, then he goes to a car lot and tries to buy some of them from a salesman there. The forger tells the salesman that he is selling cars out of his house, and needs some contracts to help make the sales go easier. If the salesman will not sell the forger any contract books, he will most likely be able to direct him to a place where they can be purchased. Some office-supply outlets sell different versions of this type of contract. If the forger can find a place that sells them this way, he just uses a typewriter or a rubber stamp (one can get them made at many places) and puts a business name on the top of the contracts. A name on the top of the contracts makes them look better when reselling the vehicles, but if the forger is doing everything the way he is supposed to, it is not that important in the long run.

The forger fills out the blank contract and title with the correct information about the vehicle. The VIN (vehicle identification number) is on the dashboard or the doorjamb, and the rest of the information on the contract is pretty simple to figure out for himself. The forger will also need a regular type of *Receipt Book* for making out a phony receipt for the transaction of buying the vehicle from the original dealership. He uses a cashier's check as the source of payment, since large amounts of cash are suspect in most transactions of this amount. The numbers or the name of the bank can be anything the forger wants. He would not have the vehicle if the check were not good, so the forger doesn't worry about that angle. Most transactions of this amount will have the following: a sales contract; a title; a receipt for the original sale of the vehicle; and the registration the forger got from the state when he registered the vehicle. The forger will simply create all but the registration, and that will come from the state in which he is legally selling the vehicle. If the forger puts the sales tax amount in the correct place on the sales contract, he can avoid having to pay anything when he registers the vehicle (except the registration fee of usually less than a hundred dollars). If the forger needs the tax amount for the contract, he can call any dealership in that area and they will tell him the amount he can expect to pay when he buys a vehicle. The forger will call as many dealerships as it takes to get all of the information he needs for the contracts; they are the best source of current information, and when doing fraud crimes it is always advisable to use the most reliable sources of information possible. If the forger acts like a potential customer, the dealerships will tell him anything that they think might make him come to them for a sale. This is an important source of information, so the facile forger will make use of it.

Next, the forger goes to his state's Department of Motor Vehicles and registers the vehicle under one of his fake names. If the forger acts like a person who is doing this service for the owners of vehicles who are too busy to do it themselves, he can have the wrong paperwork or not enough paperwork, and the clerk will just tell him to go and get what he needs and return later to register the vehicle. This method of registering a vehicle allows one to make mistakes that are covered by the excuse: *"This is all that the owner gave me. Let me call or go and get the correct information for you, and I will return later."* The forger can make all of the mistakes he wants and not raise any suspicions. The service that the forger says he is providing can be a business or just a favor for a friend, since both are done all of the time in the registration of vehicles and other matters that demand a long line or a waiting period. If the paperwork is even close, the forger will get the car registered. It is really very easy to do once the forger gets over the fear of thinking that the forces of law and order are waiting in the wings to arrest him the moment he makes a mistake. The Department of Motor Vehicles has no reason to suspect the forger of any wrongdoing, so he should just act normal. If the forger ever feels the need to regroup, he need merely walk out and go to another DMV, or return the next day. They won't care one way or the other, because they are too busy to give a hoot. If the forger has to go to every DMV in the city, then he does so. This is a job, and the forger is getting paid very well to do it, so he treats it as such. The vehicles the forger will be working with will not be reported stolen until much later, and he is just "doing this for a friend" anyway. The forger can use the same ID for all of the vehicles if he doesn't waste time. If time becomes a problem, he just calls up the agencies and extends his rental periods. This is one of the beauties of this scam; there are no stolen vehicles to report, so the forger is never in jeopardy while doing it. If the forger uses different IDs in each city, the magnitude of the crime will most likely be overlooked by each city's law enforcement authorities. This may not seem like a big deal, but the fewer police agencies working on the case, the better off the forger will be in the long run. There is a vehicle stolen every 17 seconds in this country, so the forger's plan is to not stand out in this common occurrence, so that his crime will be just another statistic that no one has time to worry about.

Now that the forger has license plates and registrations to match his vehicles and ID, it's time to sell or borrow against the vehicle. If the forger wants to, he can do both at the same time in the same city. The forger merely makes up more than one set of ownership papers for the vehicles with which he wants to do more than one deal. The forger goes to as many banks as he can find that will make him a collateralized loan on the vehicle, and he is in business. The banks will want to see the vehicle before they make the loan, but that's not a problem, since the forger will not be giving the car to anyone until he has all of the deals lined up to happen within a few days from the beginning of his scam. The banks mail the lien notices to the appropriate state agency, so the forger will have three or four days from the time he actually surrenders the title to the bank before the shit hits the fan. Three banks per vehicle is not pushing it, and it's less than one day's work. When the forger makes arrangements to sell one of the vehicles through the paper or by any advertised means, he always takes the vehicle to the potential buyer. That way, they never get to see the forger's base of operations, nor another vehicle. If the forger is pressed for time, he can always sell the vehicles at a car lot or auto auction. He acts the part of a man who is going through a divorce and needs quick cash before the judge gives the ex-wife everything he has worked hard for. The forger can also use the bankruptcy excuse, too; most salespeople are male, and if they think that they are helping a fellow male to get the best of a woman or the courts, they will bend over backwards to help. The forger plays the role that the audience will accept, usually with successful results. Most people have sold cars before; it really is no big deal. The forger is selling a vehicle for which he has all of the legally issued paperwork, and it is registered with plates and title, so he acts like a regular person instead of a crook.

If the forger really wants to do this scam big-time, then he can do it with motor homes. Their value is substantially more than other vehicles, and his return will be greater for the same amount of effort and time. Since the forger has the opportunity for a really large score, he takes the time to set it up correctly. As an example, the forger can setup a motor-home rental business in a different state, and with a little paperwork manipulation can then sell or borrow against the entire business at one time. The forger does not have to have twelve motor homes to *appear* to have them; the paperwork can show that they are out on rental whenever the lenders come by to see him. It is expected that some of them would be gone from the lot on any regular business day, so it would seem normal to anyone stopping by. The mere appearance of owning ten or twelve motor homes is justification for a two or three hundred thousand dollar loan from most banks. The true value would be around half a million dollars, so the loan-to-value ratio is very acceptable to most lenders. This is a very easily done scam, and even if it takes the forger several months to set up correctly, he is way ahead of the game financially when the smoke clears. If this seems too intense, then the forger just treats the motor homes like less expensive vehicles and sells or borrows against them. Two motor homes are equivalent to half a dozen cars in terms of dollars, so the forger will oftentimes try his hand at the simpler scam until his confidence is where it needs to be to do more. This is a very sweet crime, and there is little in the way of deterrents from the law to foil the forger.

There are many variations of the vehicle-title plan, if the forger has the paperwork angle covered, so he concentrates on getting the basics of creating documents down and is then in a great position to try some of them. Many forgers concentrate on vehicle-title fraud if check fraud is beyond their capabilities. Vehicle-title fraud requires less public contact, and the penalties are not that severe. I have been forging vehicle titles in one form or another for over twenty years, and the only major difference today is that the current technology makes it a lot easier. If the forger is interested in other sorts of crimes, the vehicle-rental part of this scam is a good way to acquire the vehicles needed for doing them. If the forger has to abandon the vehicle for any reason, he is out little. The forger can also wash the title through several states in order to keep the vehicle and use it for himself if he so desires.

Chapter Twelve

The Bonded Credit Card

This is one of the most important tools in the business, so the forger must become familiar with obtaining them and always have several, along with ID to match, in case of an emergency. Bonded credit cards are offered by plenty of banks across the country, and ads are always running on television for more and more banks that offer them. Most of the places that make them available nowadays are interested only in the deposit that the cardholder must make, so the requirements for getting them are easily met. If a paycheck stub is requested, the forger can supply all that are needed with a push of a button. If the bank requests a photo of the forger's drivers license, he can send them anything he wants to, or he can just offer the explanation that his license has been suspended. They will take a notarized statement and a copy of the forger's birth certificate as additional verification. If the bank requests a Social Security number, then the forger sends them one that matches an ID setup he has. The worst thing that the bank can do is refuse to do business with the forger, so he tries as many banks as he wants to until he has the needed cards. As long as the bank has the forger's deposit, it feels protected. Giving the forger a card is no big deal to them. Anyone who has ever applied for such a card knows what I mean. It is easy to get several cards from the same bank if the forger uses different addresses and names. The banks do not compare pictures or anything like that. If anyone comes snooping around getting information on the forger after he has used a card, the most they will get is a bad picture of him. When the forger sends them a photocopy of something with his picture on it, he tries to make the image of himself look as bad as possible. If the bank will not accept it, then the forger tries another bad one until they do, or until someone else does. Photocopies of photographs are usually terrible anyway, so the forger makes it bad, but not too bad.

Acquiring bonded credit cards is easy, and having them and using them is a must for most types of fraud crimes. They are an important tool that the forger will be hard-pressed to do without, so he takes the time to learn how to get them.

There is a space on the application that allows the forger to get a second card for someone else. If he gives the bank another name, they will send him another card with that name on it as well. This kills two birds with one stone. These cards are a very good way to launder money; they will accept a substantial amount of money towards the forger's card's credit limit. If the forger uses the card for most of his living expenses, he will be able to carry less cash on his person when traveling or shopping.

With a credit card and drivers license, the forger can look normal while doing almost anything. When renting vehicles, checking into hotels, or doing any other normal, middle-class activities, a credit card gives the impression of stability and credibility, both of which are important to the person living under an assumed identity. The prudent forger will get several cards under his permanent (new) identity as well. The forger's fraudulent credit report under his new, assumed name, will appear better to those who may be looking. The forger can also bond a Gold Card, and several of these are really good at solving life's little problems. There is no one to question the forger's having fifteen or twenty thousand dollars tied up in bonded cards. It's probably something that would never come up anyway, but it's nice to have the cushion of the cash as a backup in case the forger ever needs to run away and hide. I cannot stress how important these cards are to people in this line of work. They help create the illusion needed for doing crime and living before and after the crimes are done. The forger can have as many cards as he wants, as long as he pays his bills on time. The banks don't care one way or the other.

Chapter Thirteen

Alternative Identification

This chapter is about an essential component of the forger's arsenal: fake ID. The forger will have to use and lose several ID setups for each scam that he does. He must acquire the skills and knowledge needed to obtain what is required in the ID department before attempting anything else. The forger will need to pick up more advanced publications designed to further his education in the ID department. There are several methods of obtaining legally issued, totally valid ID setups. The methods that are explained here are only some of the many that the forger uses to obtain drivers licenses and state ID cards, which will enable him to obtain Social Security numbers and passports, if he wishes. They are the methods which are preferred by many forgers, but they may not suit the fledgling forger's abilities. Further study may be required if the forger wishes to pursue this line of work.

The computer and scanner setup described earlier in this book will give the forger the ability to make all of the documents needed to acquire new ID. If he obtains the notary stamps or seals, the forger can easily provide the paperwork that is required by the state agencies which supply drivers licenses and identity cards. It is a simple matter to use the photo credit card for supporting ID documentation that is often requested when one is obtaining a new drivers license or ID card. These methods are what the forger uses for getting legally issued ID setups.

They are the only way to go, so the forger doesn't waste his time with anything else.

There is a very simple way that the forger can get a state-issued drivers license or identity card. There is no way of guaranteeing which one he will walk out of the DMV with, but either one is fine for his purposes. If the forger obtains only the identity card, he can easily trade it up for a drivers license at a later date of his choosing. Which one of the two forms of ID the forger gets is based on his ability to persuade the clerk giving him the card that the forger needs the drivers license so desperately that the clerk feels the need to give it to him. The basic identity card is actually sufficient for most of the forger's needs, but the drivers license is always preferred and should be obtained if possible. Taking the driver's test is a requirement that the forger should be capable of passing. If not, his career choice needs to be reevaluated.

This might sound a little on the crazy side, but it is surely a viable (and almost guaranteed) way to get new ID. I have done it many times, and have never been refused. It is the only way that I or most other forgers acquire the new ID setups anymore. One of the other benefits of using this method is that it requires no supporting documents at the initial stage, and most of the time none during the second, either. If an additional piece of documentation is requested by the DMV, a *certified* (notarized) copy of the forger's birth certificate will more than suffice in most cases. If the forger has trouble at one DMV branch, then he goes to one of the many others that most cities have. The other real plus to this method is that it is virtually unstoppable by any type of law enforcement. There are so many police officers coming and going in the cop business that the odds of the forger encountering one who has had this scam pulled on him before are a million to one at best. And besides, the forger is not really doing anything to make himself memorable anyway.

First, the forger dresses nicely and acts casual. He goes to a place that has a lot of people, such as a mall or a fair or carnival. All work very well, but, if given a choice, I choose the carnival, and do it at night. The forger finds a real policeman (not a Rent-a-Cop), and acts upset, telling the cop that he has just been robbed by someone who grabbed his wallet and then ran off toward parts unknown. The forger acts a little upset, but not frantic. If the forger acts like a victim, most cops will be sympathetic, even if they would rather be doing something else. They will do what they have been trained to do: serve and protect the public. The cop will then ask the forger for his name, address, and other personal information that he needs to complete the all-important *police report*. The police officer will accept all that the forger says as fact, without questioning it. After all, the forger is the victim, and the police are trained to treat victims with compassion and respect in situations such as this. As long as the forger doesn't claim to have been physically attacked by the thief, the police officer will not call for an ambulance or other support personnel. This is a game, but it is a serious game, so the forger never halts his act in the middle, or else he will cause himself some major heartaches.

The forger must convince a policeman that he has been robbed of his identification, in order to obtain a copy of the subsequent police report.

Now, with a copy of the magical police report in hand, the forger goes to the DMV and explains what has happened to the nice public servant who handles his request. The forger says that he needs an ID of some kind in order to begin the process of acquiring new credit cards to replace those which have been stolen, and for checking into a hotel. The forger acts helpless and victimized, and explains to the person helping him that he cannot even check into a hotel without proper identification, and that the forger is starting to fall apart because of this incident. The forger mentions a good local hotel and has the number handy so that he can ask the DMV person to call the hotel on his behalf. It is unlikely that the DMV person will call for the forger, but even if he does, he will find out that 99.9% of this country's hotels will not accept a registration without some ID, and the forger's credibility and vulnerability will only increase when they learn this. The whole idea here is to get the DMV to give the forger what he wants, so the forger says and does whatever he thinks is necessary to achieve this. There are many aspects to the forger's becoming a successful con man and thief, and convincing people to grant his requests is only one of them. The aspiring forger must get comfortable with face-to-face lying and spontaneous story-creating, as they are the cornerstones of a successful white-collar criminal career, and will be needed in most of the crimes discussed in this book.

Since the forger will tell the DMV that he is from another state, his name will not be expected to be in the DMV computer *(very important),* so the DMV will probably try to issue the forger a state ID card. This is as good as a drivers license for most purposes, but if the forger tells the DMV that he needs a drivers license so that he can rent a car for his business appointments and to get around the city, there is a good chance that the DMV will let the forger take the written driving test right then, and then let the forger have a license. These are extenuating circumstances, and it is surprising what can be accomplished if one tries. If the DMV will give the forger only an ID card, then he must be gracious and return the next day to take the driving test.

When the forger returns, his new name will be in the computer, so he is already halfway there. It is important that the forger not fail the test more than two or three times. The important thing for the forger to remember is that the reason he does not have any other supporting documents is because he was robbed, and he was told by the police that the police report would solve all of his problems. The forger asks the DMV to call the police department and ask for the officer who took his report: *"He said to have them call if there were any problems."* When the forger throws this into the DMV's face, it is very unlikely that the call will be made, and even more unlikely that the officer who took the report in the evening will be on duty in the daytime. Even if the DMV calls the forger's bluff, he has little to fear and nothing to lose.

Most people cringe when faced with the possibility of confronting a cop, and the fear of blatantly lying to them is what keeps most people from using this method of obtaining new "legal" ID. All of this is very simple, and once the forger has done this himself, he will realize just how easy it can be. Many aspiring forgers will opt for another method, and this is a shame, because no other way of getting ID is as simple as this one. I have never failed to get an ID in this way. I once had to go to another DMV, which took almost ten whole minutes, because I had a clerk that I couldn't work with. But he didn't stop me; he just delayed the inevitable for a few minutes. I won because I was persistent, and I didn't accept *"No!"* for an answer. The forger must learn that *"No!"* is usually used in place of *"I am afraid to make a decision on my own."* People who take orders for a living seldom use their own free will in decision-making. Patience and diligence are necessary in any successful business venture, legal or otherwise. The astute forger will practice these attributes in his work, and try not to act too surprised when things go his way.

When the need for short-term, disposable ID is felt by the forger, the following method works quite well. It means actually getting a license that belongs to someone else who is in the DMV computer of the state the forger is getting the ID in. This way has its pros and cons. The pro is that the forger saves a step in the ID-card-to-drivers-license process, and he gets a valid license right away. The con is that the forger gets a license that someone else is driving around with at the same time as he. There is a slim possibility that the forger might encounter a problem, but he knows the possibility exists, so he deals with it. The real owner of the drivers license might also have a problem with his Social Security number which might prevent the forger from opening a bank account for cashing checks, but since the forger can get several different IDs from different DMV offices, he can always just change to an unencumbered ID that will work perfectly well. This concept is not nearly as confusing as it may seem. The successful forger is intelligent enough to grasp the basics of the scam under discussion, and is resourceful enough to know where to get his questions answered.

To get the actual paperwork that the forger will need to do this type of ID setup, he will have to visit one of the information-storage facilities that all government offices make available to those seeking such information. These facilities are a treasure-trove of information on the forger's fellow man, and they are free. They have copies of all of the documents that are used in conducting business on any normal day. These documents contain full names, addresses, dates of birth, physical descriptions, Social Security numbers, and some even have the names of relatives (and information about them, too). These storage facilities go by a host of different names, but the average Joe calls them *dumpsters*. The dumpsters used by the DMV and the Office of Vital Statistics are gold mines of information for fraud crimes. They contain carbon copies and discarded originals of applications for licenses, birth certificates, and a slew of other bullshit that the system needs to keep track of citizens. Since dumpster-diving is a business endeavor for a lot of street people and aluminum-can collectors, the forger dresses accordingly and takes a sack along on his foraging expeditions. Dumpster-diving is almost fun, and the stuff that the forger salvages will unfailingly blow his mind. Drivers licenses have physical descriptions and dates of birth on them. The forger merely finds one that matches his general description and age, and he is on the fast track to criminal success. Oftentimes, if the forger kills an hour prospecting in the proper dumpster, he will find ten such documents that will work for him. He uses that information when he plays his trick on the cop, because it will already be in the DMV's computer. The forger will also be able to tell the DMV clerk that he was recently in on the date that the carbon or application states, and that he cannot believe that he needs to replace the damn thing so soon. He suggests to the DMV that it would be nice if he didn't have to pay again; after all, he was robbed. In most cases, the clerk will have sympathy for the forger as a victim, and even though they do have to charge him again, the clerk will make the ordeal easier. Hard or easy, the forger will still get the ID, and that translates into a job well done.

When dealing with various government offices, the forger must remember that some states are different, but in general the rules are more or less the same. These are rules, not practices. The differences in the way the offices are run are astounding. There is absolutely no consistency in their procedures. What won't work at one place will most likely work at another, or another, or another. It's rather like asking people to dance; the first one might say yes, but then again they might say no. If one wants to dance badly enough, one will ask more than one person. A negative response only means that one did not say or do what that person needed to hear or see in order to satisfy their requirements. Normal people have often been informed by bank or DMV personnel that their requests cannot be honored because of faulty paperwork or signatures. These people didn't blow a whistle, or try to tackle the law-abiding citizen as he left. They simply went on to the next person in line and forgot about the problematic one. Such clerks say *"No!"* to a hundred people a day; it's part of their exciting careers. The forger need simply ask these clerks what it will take to satisfy them, and then he will know how to play it the next time. If the scam goes down without a hitch, the forger will be like the hundreds of other people who they helped that day and sent on their way. These people are civil servants and low-paid employees, and processing such requests is what they do in their jobs. They are not the F.B.I., so the forger can take his time and practice this deception at as many places as it takes to accomplish his goals.

One final point: the forger does not get fake ID in states which mail the ID, since his photo will be kept on file and he will need a real address to receive the ID.

Chapter Fourteen
Insurance Fraud

Insurance fraud is not going to make the forger rich, but it is a good short-term cure for financial problems, and it is by far the easiest form of fraud. If the forger is not a homeowner, or a tenant who has been at the same place for a long time with insurance on his possessions, then he must pass on this particular crime. If the forger meets the above requirements, this type of crime is almost impossible to solve, and he should be able to collect a tidy sum if he sets it up correctly.

The forger's policy is the key to the whole scam, so he gives it a good going-over so that he fully understands exactly what is required and covered. Most normal policies have fixed amounts for basic possessions, such as electronics, clothing, guns, jewelry, and other normally owned items. The forger will need to make sure that he spreads out his loss, or else he will run into a wall concerning the amount of coverage he has on particular items. If the forger sticks to the basic burglary profile, the process will be quick and simple. The forger reports the crime, the police come out and make a report. The forger contacts the insurance company, they verify the crime. The forger collects on his loss. It's simple.

There is a residential burglary in this country every 15 seconds, and the forger's scam will just be another statistic. All he has to do is fake a break-in, lie about what has been stolen, and collect his check. It will be an additional opportunity for the forger to play the victim, but it's really no big deal to anyone, especially the cops. If the forger does not have additional coverage for more expensive belongings, he has the choice of collecting the amount of his current coverage, or adding coverage and waiting another six months to file the claim. The difference can be substantial, so if the forger can wait, then he should do so. If not, he can purchase the additional coverage after the first break-in, and do it again the following year. He might piss off the insurance company, but the return is worth the hassle. This is by far the easiest crime that the forger will ever do, and it pays quite well for being virtually idiot-proof.

The following things are not just important for the forger to keep in mind; they are absolutely critical!

1. The forger must not tell anyone his intentions. His wife or girlfriend will see that he is padding the claim, but she doesn't need to know that the forger faked the crime. The forger needn't exclude his female companion, but he doesn't want her to have any knowledge that can ever be used against him if she someday gets angry or wants a divorce. It's the forger's call, but he does not need any help at the crime scene, and he never knows how she might hold up to police questioning. If the forger is slick, he can both do the crime without her knowledge and be with her when the "break-in" is discovered. The forger can meet her someplace that she can go to directly from another place; she should not go there directly from their home. This gives him time to make the break-in look convincing, and then meet her so that the two of them can return home later and discover the crime. If the forger cannot keep his mouth shut forever, at least her knowledge will be hearsay at best, and a good lawyer might get him off if it ever comes to that.

2. Insurance companies always ask for receipts for one's possessions when a burglary has taken place, and since the forger is going to lie about what has been stolen, it's unlikely that he will have all of the receipts the insurance company wants. So, to solve this problem, the forger just tells the police and the insurance company that all of his personal papers (receipts included) were kept in a small, portable, fireproof lockbox. Since this box was also taken in the

crime, the forger cannot provide any receipts for his purloined possessions. This will not sound as strange as one might think it does, and besides, this is probably the forger's first claim with this insurance company. Who's going to call him a liar? Most middle-class Americans have the same sorts of possessions in their homes, and the insurance company has a pretty good idea of what those things are, based on statistical analysis. The forger's loss will be no different than most, with a few exceptions that will guarantee his collection of a decent amount. Twenty or thirty grand is not a far-fetched figure for this primitive sort of fraud. The average middle-class home burglary results in a loss of almost fifteen thousand dollars, and with a little jewelry and a few electronic items added in, the forger's claim will seem reasonable. The forger knows that he does not get what he does not ask for.

3.　The forger will kick open his back or garage door, and move a few things around that might have been in the way when it was supposedly done. Or, maybe the forger will make it appear that the entry was gained through a window. There will be no fingerprints if gloves were used, and the authorities will assume that gloves were used anyway, so the absence of prints is reasonable and explainable. The forger doesn't need to make a big mess; that's TV, not reality. Most thieves come in, steal the same items, and leave without doing much real damage to the premises. The cops know this, and so does the forger. He turns out a *few* dresser drawers, and leaves some big, heavy items such as stereo speakers by a back door, as if they were left behind for some unknown reason. If the forger uses a window for the fictitious point of entry, he messes up the ground outside the window a little bit. Cops tend to notice these things. Also, if the forger kicks down a door, he wears a pair of shoes which are a couple of sizes larger than his own that he picked up in a second-hand store. He might leave a few footprints outside a window, to make it appear that the burglar peered in before he broke into the house. It's the little things that make the difference, so the forger thinks like a burglar when he creates his false scenario. Of course, the forger can always just say that he left the door unlocked. It is not a crime to do so, and it will not affect the claim.

4. The forger buys (and returns later) or borrows a couple of shotguns or rifles that he can lean against a wall to have in the background of a picture he takes of a friend or wife. This is the kind of evidence that he can show the insurance adjuster to help convince him of the forger's honesty when he lists what was taken. If the forger's policy has only a small amount of coverage on weapons, the forger acquires and photographs what he thinks will be needed to max out that particular coverage. The forger makes sure that he tells the police about the guns, as most rifles and shotguns are not registered, and his will be no different. The forger can expect a lecture from the cops about firearms registration. The forger explains that he had the serial numbers and paperwork on the guns in the lock box, and since he has had the weapons for years, attempting to trace the record of his purchases is futile.

5. The forger goes to several computer stores and buys a few bucks worth of junk that is associated with computers. It has to look as if he had a computer sitting somewhere. Few crooks take everything a computer has sitting around it. The forger makes the place where the stolen computer sat look realistic, as the police aren't all idiots. He can pick up a few empty computer boxes at any computer store, and they can be stored somewhere in the house. The forger can feign looking at the empty boxes for additional information on the expensive computer setup he recently purchased. The forger's computer might be included in his electronics coverage. If it is, then his stereo gear will probably more than burn that coverage up. The forger can always call his insurance company a few weeks before the break-in and add coverage for his new computer. This is totally normal, and ensures that the computer will be fully covered.

6. When the forger stashes the missing items that he actually does own, he doesn't get radical about hiding them. No one is likely to search his house or the trunk of his car. The forger cleans up and rearranges things, since he is not expected to leave everything the way he found it for the insurance adjuster to see. The forger

doesn't take things to a friend's place or to a neighbor's; it looks suspicious, to say the least.

7. The forger doesn't forget his leather coats and other expensive items of clothing. He is trying to cover all of the areas of his policy, especially if he does not have replacement coverage. The forger's allowance for clothing is probably a thousand dollars; that is a common amount. His policy will have all of the figures with which he needs to work.

8. If the forger has replacement coverage, he doesn't overlook the many portable items that a good policy covers. A portable computer, golf and scuba equipment, binoculars, camera gear, and a violin or guitar are all common. Stamp collections and power or hand tools are both very normal and costly. There is nothing that the forger cannot claim to have had stolen if he prepares correctly. This crime can net a sizable reward if the forger takes the time to do it right. Why would he do it any other way?

9. The forger is mindful that he is a victim who has been paying his policy premiums for years to cover just such an event. He acts like he is supposed to, and doesn't beg for anything that he has coming to him. The forger expects to be reimbursed, and he lets the insurance company know that he does.

Chapter Fifteen

Making One's Own Credit Cards

The credit card may seem like a difficult item to copy, but if the forger has the same equipment as the companies who make the cards, it can be very simple. It's the acquisition and use of that equipment that will be covered in this chapter. For the forger, making his own credit cards is more or less the same as making his own documents. He obtains correct tools, and the job is virtually done. The tools for making credit cards are for sale to anyone who wishes to possess them, as are the tools for making documents, and there are no restrictions on getting or owning them.

Credit cards are manufactured by several methods. The basic process is simple: take a piece of plastic, attach a magnetic strip on the back, cover both sides with printing, and then melt the name and number of the owner into the card. In some cases, the forger can and will put the photo of the owner on the card as well. This may seem complicated, but the forger can buy the blank cards with the magnetic strips already on them. By attaching a machine smaller than a regular toaster to his computer, the forger can print information and photos onto the blank cards with a few minutes of preparation and practice. Then, with another small machine (which is not attached to the computer), the forger can emboss (melt) the name and numbers right into the card where they belong. Sounds a lot simpler already, doesn't it? It really is a good and simple way to accomplish a lot of things besides just copying someone else's credit cards. A credit card with the forger's photograph on it and a birth certificate will get him a new ID setup in nothing flat.

None of the things discussed here are revelations or deeply guarded secrets. They are just common sense applied to a particular problem. Like most situations in this business, if the forger treats them in a businesslike way, the mystery becomes nothing more than just learning how to get the tools and do the job correctly. If the forger wanted to become a rocket scientist, he would go to rocket-scientist school. If the forger wanted to branch out and become a burglar, he would attend locksmith and alarm schools. The process should be education first, and then the perpetration of the crime, but in most situations in the crime field, it's usually the other way around. Most people think that crime is something that anybody can do successfully with little or no training, and beginners fail every day, disproving that theory. It amazes me that most of the "criminals" I meet in and out of prison always blame someone, or something, for their own lack of skill and training. No one is born with knowledge, so why would anyone presume to have it when it's obvious that he does not? If the forger wants to do fraud as a way to make money, he must have the tools and knowledge. Otherwise, he is just asking for failure and trouble. If the forger wants to do this type of thing for a living, then he must pay strict attention and not take any shortcuts when assessing the requirements for the tasks at hand.

Making credit cards is actually a lot easier than making documents, and no special skill is needed. The forger must, however, have the capacity to follow instructions that a computer will provide him if he asks for it. Most computers will walk the user through the processes necessary to achieve his goals, and the credit-card setup is no different. A little practice will suffice for this particular crime. The steps are simple and the computer is designed to help the beginner learn the process. In a matter of hours, the determined forger will know all that there is to know about the machine and its workings and capabilities.

There are several places to go to get the equipment to make one's own credit cards — just check the Yellow Pages under "Embossing Equipment & Supplies." The forger can get what he wants from these companies — they deal with hundreds (or even thousands) of customers daily, and the forger is just another customer to them. Anyone who wants to get involved in selling and manufacturing credit card-like products (such as bank cards, ID cards, parking-garage cards, phone cards, etc.) will turn to these companies for equipment and supplies.

For the forger, setting up his own business to do this requires only an hour or so of his time and a couple hundred bucks of his money. Once the forger has established a business entity, the embossing equipment companies will not only sell him the things he needs, but they will help him understand how to use it. They have support departments, and a phone call is all that is required to get a problem solved. All major cities have embossing equipment companies with showrooms, and all the forger has to do is call up one and ask to see the latest plastic-card system they have for sale. The forger tells them that he wants to make and sell phone cards, parking-garage access cards, or anything along those lines. The salesman might ask the forger to come in so that he can show the forger all kinds of great stuff. The forger will not be expected to know anything, since he is a beginner in the business. A good salesman will sense the forger's keen interest, and, anticipating a commission as a result of selling some expensive equipment, will help the forger understand what he can actually do with the embossing equipment company's materials to generate money for his new business. The forger supplies the interest, and the embossing equipment company supplies the knowledge and equipment. After all, their business success necessitates that new customers, such as the deceptive forger, buy and use their products.

It takes about twenty thousand dollars to purchase the minimum equipment required to do this right. Although this money will be well spent, there are few who will part with even a portion of that amount if there is another way to get the equipment. The forger who is less concerned with what is right and wrong in the *physical* crime department will employ the methods outlined in Chapter 18, which explores an alternative method of getting started, along with the more widely accepted method.

I will continue my description of the forger's activities, based on the assumption that he has obtained the necessary equipment and is ready to get started.

Since all that the forger will really be doing is making himself a copy of someone else's legally obtained and currently valid credit card, the first thing he will need to address is getting the necessary information to duplicate another person's card. The best and most dependable form of this information is a copy of the user's card. The good news is that every time a card is used, a copy is created. It is true that there is a growing awareness of what is done with the copies produced from credit-card usage, but, as usual, the response generated by this awareness is mostly half-assed. Many clerks don't bother to destroy credit-card copy slips, but routinely toss them into the trash, with a mindless disregard for the privacy and/or security of the credit-card user. The forger often concentrates on restaurants, because they are a veritable gold mine for the type of credit-card information that the forger is seeking to acquire, e.g., *American Express* (because they have no set limit) and any *Gold Card* (for obvious reasons).

The forger can make and use any card currently in circulation, but he must be aware of the card's limits in order to get a decent return on his investment of time. If the forger puts his photo on the card, as many card issuers now do, he can avoid the secondary ID problem that sometimes accompanies large purchases. Since new cards are being introduced into the marketplace every day, the forger can put his picture on any card, and it will be accepted. When the card number is run for verification, it will clear. The card with the photo is the industry's latest attempt to foil credit-card fraud, but the technology used to add the photo has been available for years. I have been putting pictures on various types of credit cards and access cards since 1992, and it is a simple process with the equipment the embossing equipment companies sell as an addition to their credit-card systems. They will sell the forger anything he asks for, since there are no restrictions on owning and operating such equipment. A business license is not required to buy from the embossing equipment company, but it is a good cover for the forger, and avoids unwanted speculation.

The equipment needed for this work consists of a regular personal computer, a scanner, a printer, a camera and an embosser. All of the necessary software programs are already in the computer, which is set up to do what the forger wants. He just turns the computer on and makes cards! The scanner is used to copy the cards the forger wants to duplicate. He scans any real credit card into the computer, and then changes the information until he gets the name and numbers that he wants to print. Once the forger scans say, a VISA card into the computer, he will always have it in the database for future use. The machine will produce a finished card that looks like the original one, with the exception of the embossed name and numbers. The forger then puts the card into the embosser and melts the name and numbers into it. The holographic image is reproduced when the forger scans and prints the card. The hologram may not be perfect, but it looks realistic and the card will clear, which eliminates suspicion. The forger can even purchase *different* holographic stickers to put onto the cards. They look exactly like the real thing, but are not the same image. Try your memory right now: what image is on your VISA card? No one else is likely to know, either, and the clerks who glance at the forger's fake credit card are certainly not going to interfere with a customer who merely wants to spend money.

The only real glitch that the forger will encounter is not really a problem, just an inconvenience that the clerk will quickly solve. The magnetic strip on the back of the phony card will not work when the cashier runs the card through the machine. This is due to the fact that there is no information encoded into that strip. Many valid cards do not register, so the clerk will just punch in the numbers manually. In some cases, a clerk may even take the time to inspect the card to see if they can clean it up and try again. This is because they are too lazy to type the numbers in, not because they think there is anything wrong with the card. The forger can make a few scratches on the magnetic strip with his thumbnail ahead of time, and this will appear to be the reason for the card's malfunction, if the clerk bothers to look, which is unlikely. It is a common occurrence for a credit card's magnetic strip to malfunction; that is why there is a manual keypad.

Embossing equipment companies supply credit-card stock in a variety of colors and formats. They even sell card stock in different colors, just like most of the credit cards in use today. The "designer" card is the industry's latest innovation. These cards are the perfect cover for the forger to practice and display his creativity. There is no way for the merchant to verify the design. As long as the numbers come back OK, the merchant will just accept it and complete the transaction. If a card has a photo on it, the merchant will be even more at ease. If the card's account has reached its limit, the phony card will be rejected just like a real card. The forger will be informed that his purchase cannot be completed because the card is maxed out, *nothing more*. If the forger is using a phony American Express or any Gold Card, he has no limit to worry about. He just limits himself to a couple of heavy shopping days, and doesn't get greedy.

Another very good way to use the credit-card making equipment is for obtaining ID. If the forger takes a credit card with his name and photo on it into a Department of Motor Vehicles service office, he can use it to get a state-issued ID card with surprising ease. If the forger wants to cover all of his bases and not have to rely so heavily on his bullshitting ability, then he takes a birth certificate (self-notarized) along with him, too. The forger sometimes creates the paperwork for a false police report, and brings that along with his fake credit-card backup. There are several ways that the forger can provide the documentation needed for obtaining additional identity cards. The key to this method of getting new ID is to ask for it, nothing more. This method of obtaining ID is seldom employed, because most people consider it too difficult or outright impossible. I use no other method, because this is by far the best way of obtaining what I need. Once the forger has the state ID card, he just returns another day to take the test to get his driver's license. This is an easy way to get all of the IDs he wants, and sometimes the forger is tempted to do this for other people.

Unless the forger is getting paid *very well*, he is foolish to fall victim to this seemingly easy method of supplying ID to those who ask him for a favor. The odds are that someone will get busted, and the forger's problems will then come from a direction he is not prepared for. This is a sophisticated enough crime that the knowledge of it can be used as a bargaining chip by someone else who has been busted and is willing to save his or her ass by giving up the forger's. The forger mustn't be naïve enough to believe that people can be trusted. Partners are to help spend the forger's money and then rat him off. If the forger keeps this scam to himself, he can make all of the money he wants without creating liabilities he cannot control. This is also a business of survival. If the forger swims alone, his odds of getting pulled down are much lower, and his profits are enhanced.

Remember

1. If the forger dresses and acts like a businessman, he will be treated like one.
2. If one source won't sell the forger the equipment that he wants, he simply goes to another one. DMV service offices are everywhere, too.
3. The forger must never use stolen credit cards. One card's profits are hardly worth the risk.
4. The forger personally destroys every card he uses, and never keeps receipts.
5. The embossing equipment is very easy to use with a little practice.

Chapter Sixteen

Counterfeit Money

In the rubber-document business, sooner or later the thought of making cash will cross the forger's mind. If counterfeiting currency were as easy as it appears on television, we would be up to our asses in bad paper. Reality is very different.

For starters, cash is printed, not copied. The equipment and paper used are beyond the reach of most of the dreamers who fill our prisons. Although the technology is available, it's not worth the effort, if the forger considers the big picture when contemplating counterfeiting currency. The following example is my reason for avoiding this venture.

Let's say that the forger has everything he needs, which would include: a batch of useable paper, access to a decent offset press, the working knowledge to set up the press, and the correct ink mixture to do a *great* job. Might as well throw in Cindy Crawford as an assistant, too, but the forger wouldn't want to overreact, so we'll skip her. Anyway, let's say that the forger worked his ass off and came up with a hundred grand worth of twenty-dollar bills. We could just as easily say a million dollars worth of hundreds, but the argument is the same; the amount is not the issue. Now, the forger has a hundred grand worth of paper that is useless until he trades it for the real stuff. If the forger were to move a thousand of the bills a week, it would take him five weeks. By then, every person in the city would know what he looked like. The forger's hundred grand is now down to about seventy-five or eighty grand, if he has been lucky and hasn't lost too much in his purchase and exchange process... you know, the one he has been engaged in for the last five weeks. We won't count deductions for expenses such as food or gas; it's already too depressing. In the same amount of time, the forger could have passed a hundred grand worth of checks and spent a month in the Bahamas to boot. If not checks, then a trust-deed scam, or stocks, or bonds, or any of the other documents that have a face value higher than even a hundred-dollar bill. With the same effort it takes to convince someone to accept a bogus bill, the forger could have passed a rubber check worth ten times that amount.

Ten grand is ten checks worth a thousand dollars each. How smart does the forger have to be to see the direction I am going with this? On top of everything else, check fraud is mostly a state offense and possibly negotiable. Counterfeiting money is a federal offense with mandatory sentences which are not negotiable. If the forger has a desire to waste his time and piss off the government, why not just get a job with them and not pay his taxes?

Chapter Seventeen
The Tenant Scam

This particular scam is real-estate related, but it has so many other aspects that it should be considered just another type of fraud crime. The basic plan is to move into someone else's home as a live-in tenant, and then assume his identity so that the forger can sell or borrow against his property's equity. The forger can also get additional credit cards, or buy or lease an automobile or motor home under this person's name. The extent of what the forger can do by assuming this person's identity is wide open, and I will not cover all of the possibilities because I don't know all of them myself. This is another situation where once the forger gets his foot in the door, the rest is up to his own creativity.

This scam is like most of the others I'm explaining, and it also requires the use of disposable ID. If the forger has the false-identity area covered to the point he should have, creating documents and telling the lies that go along with them should be second nature to him by now. Let's continue with the assumption that enough has been said on that subject.

The forger usually has no trouble finding a shared-housing arrangement.

The forger should go to a newsstand and pick up several papers from cities that he wouldn't mind visiting to make a few bucks. He can look in the classified ad section under "Houses To Share," or some similar terminology. He finds the ads which imply that a professional person is looking for a roommate to share his financial burdens with. The forger calls and speaks to those who appear promising. The forger is looking for a residence that will have only the two of them living in it; no other roommates, wives, or girlfriends who don't go to work every day and leave the residence alone with only the forger home. The forger gets the address as any reputable respondent would, and tells the person that he wants to check out the neighborhood and drive by the place before he makes a decision to meet him. The forger gives the impression that he is in town, or will be shortly, and that he is moving into a new place to get a fresh start in life. (The forger also makes sure to use a blocking device on his telephone when he calls, so that he doesn't tip off the person who has a caller identification device on his telephone.) The forger needs to find several residences that seem promising, and then either go to the city and check them out for himself or have an agency do it over the phone. He needs to make sure that the residence which he is considering renting has a decent amount of equity in it before the forger wastes any more of his time on it. The address is all the forger needs in order to look at the mortgage paperwork at the courthouse. The paperwork will provide the forger with the name of the mortgage company, as well as any other debts the property has against it. The difference between the amount of the mortgage and the selling price will give the forger some idea of the equity value he will have to work with. How much equity value exists will determine whether or not this place is worth the forger's time. The forger should know that he can often borrow about 75 to 80% of the equity amount without a new appraisal or much hassle.

The forger can also have a real estate agency check out the properties he is interested in over the phone without leaving his hometown. If he calls a couple of real estate agents in the town in which he is doing crime, the forger can obtain the names of some businesses that will do such checking for a fee. The forger tells them that he is currently involved in a business deal that concerns these properties, and that he wants basic information on them that any businessman would be apt to be seeking: the mortgage amount, the balance of the mortgage, the owners' names, and any liabilities associated with the property. The forger makes arrangements to pay the real estate agents with an untraceable method such as money orders or cashier's checks which can be sent via overnight mail. It's a long shot that the forger's connection to these properties and a crime concerning them will ever be made, but he should reduce the risks whenever possible. The questions that the forger is asking are normal questions which are posed all of the time. He needn't make his inquiries seem mysterious. The forger should be able to get his answers in a couple of hours, as this process is very simple and inexpensive. There is no reason for the forger to go to the cities which don't have properties that are in his profile search, so using an agent does have a purpose. Doing so saves the forger time and energy, but it does not replace his presence in the long run. Whatever the forger's goals or expected involvement are, he must remember that the crime game is more than just a hobby, and he shouldn't expect to reap more than he is willing to sow.

Once the forger has decided on a property, he makes arrangements to move in, and tells all of the lies that are necessary to make his landlord happy. The forger is playing a role, and if he has a cell phone at his disposal he can verify any lie he tells. (See Chapter 19 for more information on how the forger does this.) If the forger pays the victim the money he is asking for, he is doing what is asked of him. The forger is solving a financial problem for the landlord. If the forger dwells on his recent divorce and his own personal reasons for wanting to move to a new place and start over, his new friend will become a person he can talk to. The forger's apparent vulnerability plays a key role in getting the victim to trust him. Doesn't everyone instinctively trust and want to help out the little puppy that seems lost or alone?

The next day, when the forger's landlord goes out to work, the forger will also go to work. The forger finds out what time the mail comes and makes a mental note to be around then and let the mailman become familiar with his retrieving the mail from his hand or the mailbox. The forger can find out a lot about his victim from the return addresses on his mail. Anything from a mortgage company or a credit card company may contain valuable information, and the forger will open and read it. The landlord need never know that this mail ever arrived. If the landlord is attempting to refinance or get new credit cards, the forger can assume his identity and use this information to his advantage. If the forger is there to receive the mail, the check that he called and directed the refinancing institution to send will arrive in his hand first. The forger will have brought the necessary materials and paperwork to fabricate ID with the landlord's name on it. How the forger does this is his business, but he will need to do it as soon as possible so that he can open up bank accounts and cash the check when it arrives. The mail will tell the forger where the landlord banks, so he merely goes to another bank to do his business. If the forger asks his victim to suggest a bank, he will most likely respond with the name(s) of the bank or banks he uses, which can then be avoided. The forger can also apply for credit cards at his new bank. Since he has credit and most banks offer their own cards, he will probably get them rather quickly.

The forger sometimes steams open his absent housemate's mail in search of pertinent financial informationl.

The resourceful forger finds a small car lot, and has the salesman run a credit check on himself (using the landlord's name), even if he has to pay for it. The forger tells the salesman that he was recently divorced, and wants to find out if his ex-wife has messed up his credit. The salesman will understand the forger's stated reasons, and will most likely do it for him. If the forger has to, he will act interested in buying a car. The report is full of information that the forger wants and needs to carry out his crime. With the credit report and the information from the mortgage paperwork in hand, the forger has all that he needs to get additional credit cards and refinance the property. Some banks offer what is known as an *Equity Credit Line*. This is basically a credit line that uses the equity in the property as collateral for any spending or cash withdrawals the property owner makes. This is actually the best way for the forger to get his hands on the equity from the property. If the forger wants to, the property can be refinanced by phone from one of the many places that advertise this service. The process of applying by phone removes all of the personal contact between the forger and a lender. All of the questions the forger has can be answered over the phone. He can call as many finance companies as he wants to. The canny forger realizes just how simple it is to refinance *any* property.

The forger can contact his landlord's mortgage company (he has learned the mortgage company's name from the victim's paperwork) and inform them that he wants to refinance, or take out a second mortgage on his property. Since the mortgage company will assume that the forger is the owner, they will do all of the necessary business over the phone. The mortgage company will already have all of the original loan information on the victim and his property in their files, so the process is very quick and hassle-free. The forger tells the mortgage company that he wishes to avoid another appraisal, and so is seeking a loan that will fit within the guidelines already established. This is normal and saves time and money, both of which are usually important to someone looking for cash from a mortgage company. If the mortgage company insists on an appraisal, the forger arranges for it to take place when the victim is working, and tells the appraiser that he wishes to keep the fact that he is borrowing money to himself, so that if the "roommate" (victim) does come home unexpectedly, he can ask the appraiser to leave and come back another time. The forger is supposed to be the owner and the *boss* of what is going on, so he gives directions and acts like someone who is in charge of the situation. The forger is not *asking* the mortgage company to loan him money; he is *giving* them the chance to make him a loan so they can make money. It's amazing how many people get the basic facts of dealing with a lender or bank backwards. The forger knows that he is the boss; he acts like it and is treated accordingly. Do you think Donald Trump *asks* for anything?

I didn't mention the check-cashing part of this scam, because it is really no different than cashing any of the checks that the forger gets from any of the scams he perpetrates. The forger should have at least a couple of weeks before anyone gets wise, and if he is at the residence to receive the payment book for the new loan when it arrives in the mail, he can stretch out the time period even longer. The forger can also purchase a car or motor home while he is waiting around. The forger will have credit, so he can take a vehicle he bought in another city and borrow against it in the victim's name at several banks in the victim's town. The forger can take the motor home or new car to another city and sell it with fake titles, or borrow against it. He can also *lease* some vehicles and sell them or borrow against them. The options are many, and the forger has the time and opportunity to do them properly. A hundred grand is not that hard to net if the forger is willing to spend a month or two on the setup.

Chapter Eighteen
The Office

Let's consider for a moment that the forger is sincere in his desire to get started in the *fraudulent document* business, but is short of the necessary funds to do so, or would rather do it without spending the serious money required. There is always a way if the desire is strong and the morals are weak. The biggest expense in setting up a professional scam (such as several mentioned in this book) is the equipment to do it. Let's look at several methods of acquiring this equipment. All of these methods require that the forger spend some money, but it will be substantially less than the twenty to twenty-five grand needed to do this legally.

The methods that make the most sense and require the least amount of violence both start out the same way. Each requires that the person who wants the equipment open up an office and set up an account with the equipment dealers. This way the dealer not only provides the needed equipment, but actually delivers it and gives a certain amount of instruction on its use. It depends on the direction that the forger is taking as to just how much further instruction he obtains, but a little is better than nothing. If the forger chooses the grab-and-go method, his instruction will be brief, but if he paid attention, he can fill in the rest with a little hands-on experience and a few phone calls to other distributors of the same equipment. If the forger chooses the second method, his instruction will be more comprehensive, but the costs will be greater because he will continue the charade a little longer. As a person who has used this equipment and taught its use to others, I can state that in most situations, a couple of days of practice are all that the forger will need to learn the use of this equipment. If a problem arises that the forger cannot solve by himself, then he can call a computer store or the embossing equipment distributors for an answer. The need to stay in contact with the supplier of this equipment is actually quite small. The forger can get supplies and parts from many other sources. This equipment is sold worldwide, and its possession is no big deal in the business world. The forger will be treated just like any other person interested in buying equipment and supplies when he deals with the many places that sell this material. All businesses need customers, and the forger is a potential customer, so he relaxes and asks questions.

The first thing that the forger needs to do is find and rent an office in a respectable part of town. An *executive suite* can be found and leased for three or four hundred dollars. The forger can go above or below that amount, but he must keep in mind that he is trying to make an impression on equipment dealers, so he shouldn't pinch pennies. The forger can feel free to sign a long-term lease, which is, of course, worth nothing if he chooses to break it. He can get a good setup this way. The forger's references can be handled by using a cell phone that has an answering recording of whatever lie he selects, or by making use of several answering services around town for a few dollars. Answering services will answer the phone any way the forger requests, and say just about anything he wants. Most high-end office complexes will make a call or two, but they really want tenants and money. If the forger tries several, greed will eventually prevail.

When the forger has his office set up and looking normal, he calls several office-supply outlets and arranges for salesmen to visit and show him a good copier and possibly a computer setup. This stuff is for rent or sale at dozens of places in the phone book. The forger lets his fingers do some walking until he has three or four who are willing to come out and try to sell or rent him something. I will provide a list of the forger's desired equipment at the end of this chapter, so, with that in mind, let's move on. After the salesmen have spent a reasonable amount of time trying to sell the forger something, he informs them that he will be in touch in a day or so and runs them off. The object is to make them wait, so that when the forger calls back with a decision they will jump at the chance to help him. The forger has them deliver the equipment with the understanding that a company check will be waiting for them.

The forger will schedule as many deliveries as he can, but doesn't have them arrive at the same time. The more equipment the forger can obtain, the more he will have to sell for working capital if he needs it later. The equipment will most likely be delivered by some delivery people who will just take the check and vanish. They would not have brought the stuff if there were any anticipated problems, so if they show up, the forger is in the game. The forger might not bat a thousand with all of the places he contacts, so he calls several, just to be sure he'll get what he needs. If the forger has any problems with getting the stuff, he can make arrangements to lease or buy the equipment over a period of time. The down payment may hurt a little, but it is easily recoverable later. If the forger chooses the grab-and-go method, he arranges the delivery times for Friday and Saturday, and is gone by the time the checks bounce on Monday.

I consider the embossing equipment to be a necessity for the perpetration of any successful fraud crime. The acquisition of this equipment is important and is given careful consideration by the knowing forger. Their equipment is the most expensive, and is key to the whole *office* scam. They will take a check for their product, just like the other places. The cost of their equipment is considerable, so the forger will spend more time with the salesman, in person and on the phone. There might be only one or two places per city where embossing equipment is available, so the forger plays it smart and doesn't rush. If cost is not an object, and the forger wants time to become familiar with using the equipment, then he makes arrangements to buy it over a period of time or lease it. Selling this stuff is the salesman's business, so he probably has several sources which will work with a reasonable down payment. This will cost the forger some cash, but it is still better than buying it all in one shot. If the forger arranges to beat several other office-supply businesses out of extra office equipment, he will be able to recover his cash outlay sooner. With the *office* as a front, the forger can have all kinds of things delivered to it, and pay for these deliveries with checks. As a going-out-of-town extra, the forger can get some items delivered on the weekend and take them with him before the banks open on Monday.

When dealing with embossing equipment companies, the forger will find it difficult to examine all of the equipment they have for sale for this type of business. The salesman will bring a condensed version to the forger's office for a demonstration. If the forger wants to see the really good stuff, he must go into their showroom for a peek. The forger will do this for a couple of reasons, the first being that he will get a thrill out of seeing the high-tech toys which are available if his pockets are deep. The second reason is the opportunity to *case* the place. It is very likely that the showroom has an alarm system, but the forger might spot a weakness which he can exploit. The forger desires all of this highly expensive equipment, and he has several options for obtaining it. If all that stood between me and several hundred grand worth of money-making toys were one or two pencil-necked geeks, it would be an easy decision. I don't advocate or recommend violence, because robbery needn't be violent if done correctly, but it is a means to an end, and the serious forger always considers it as an option. If the robbery takes place in another state and no one is hurt, it will be filed and forgotten, like the many other robberies which took place that week.

There is one other option to acquiring most of the items which the forger requires for his operation. The forger will have to buy the embossing equipment system legally, but he will have the cash from selling the extra equipment he obtained by using the above-mentioned method to work with and offset that expense. The embossing equipment is a vital component of the forger's setup because it is an important means of creating the photo credit cards which are needed to obtain additional ID setups for the forger's crimes. It can be forgone if the forger has another means of obtaining false IDs, but few methods are cleaner or quicker. The computer and related equipment are still expensive acquisitions, so the forger will sometimes consider taking a trip to another city and engaging in a little breaking and entering as a means of solving this problem. If the forger goes to another city and rents an office in a good complex with *executive suites*, he will be surrounded by offices with computer setups in each of them. These offices will contain more than enough equipment to satisfy all of the forger's needs, with plenty left over to sell, and the only thing between the forger and this equipment will be a couple of doors. How the forger deals with those doors is his business, but it sure beats armed robbery. If the forger chooses this type of equipment-gathering method, he mustn't forget to clean up after himself. A stray fingerprint would be a sloppy way to sign his work.

The following is a list of the recommended equipment the forger should try to obtain and learn to use:

1. A personal computer with at least a 386 processor. IBM format.
2. A Hewlett-Packard HPIII or equivalent, MICR-capable printer.
3. A high-resolution, optical recognition, color scanner - 600 DPI minimum.
4. Photo copier - The best one the forger can talk the salesman into selling and delivering.
5. Credit card equipment with photo capacity.
6. Laminator, embosser, camera, and plenty of blank card stock.
7. A good typewriter with changeable fonts.

Chapter Nineteen
For the Forger's Information

When applying for loans from banks or other lenders, the forger is often asked for proof of employment, income and residency. I will address these issues at this point.

The first is income, and this can be solved in two easy ways, if the forger has the equipment and common sense required. The forger tells the inquiring party (the bank) that he is self-employed and has been so for most of his life. The forger will need to create income tax statements and return forms, along with some earnings and loss statements if requested. The forger can get blank forms from almost any office-supply store, and merely doctors the dates on them to correspond with the lies he's told. The formulas and amounts are actually just figures that the forger makes up, and which add and subtract correctly on the documents to look like any other *real* tax statement. The W-2 form that a legitimate worker normally gets in the mail from an employer is easily purchased and filled out by the forger. The forger sometimes actually takes the W-2 form into a real tax preparer such as H&R Block and has it fill out the paperwork for him. Once the forger knows how to do it, he can do it for himself from then on. There is also computer software available that allows the forger to create his own tax returns from scratch. Both of the above methods supply the forger with paperwork that is almost impossible to verify. There are a couple of documents that the forger can create and *notarize* himself, and these will be accepted by 95% of the lenders out there. After all, where would a bank or anyone else call to verify the forger's fraudulent tax records? After 20 years in this business, I still don't know, and I have tried hard to find out. The lenders are obligated to accept certain pieces of paper which they require in their determination as to whether or not to make a loan. Documents which *look* official, along with a possible *notary stamp* when needed, are among these universally accepted pieces of paper. A business license can be obtained in about ten minutes at a courthouse by anyone with twenty-five bucks and a name for the business. There are few, if any, requirements for this document, yet it is one of the most important items one needs when dealing with a bank.

The other method is for the forger simply to tell the inquirer the name of his "employer," and then provide the fake documents required. The forger can use a cell phone or answering service to cover any of the lies he has told. When the lender calls the cell phone or answering service to verify the forger's information, it will get a recording or a "secretary," and will usually request a return call. The forger can then return the lender's call to complete the paperwork. The forger can also tell the "secretary" at the answering service the information he wants relayed to the lender, and she can do the job for him. Most of these places will do the forger's bidding for a fee, and he need merely look until he finds one.

Either way the forger does this, his place of employment is verified and accepted. The forger can use the second method with a landlord or mortgage company to verify his residence and provide payment records that are not in the *TRW* (or equivalent) credit bureau. The forger can setup several cell phones if he wants to, along with all of the answering services it takes to achieve his goals. Since IRS and most other tax paperwork is easy to create and tough to verify, the forger should have little trouble in his dealings with the businesses he chooses to use in the pursuit of his scams.

The forger may also want to create his own business or corporation to use for himself as his *actual* place of employment for his *real* identity. Few people have the money to retire, so the forger doesn't make himself the subject of speculation by pretending to be one of those people. If others think that the forger travels in his work, he will be more readily accepted in the community and fewer questions will be asked. The forger can set the business up in another state and pay himself a reasonable amount with a company check that he deposits in a local bank, just as if he were getting paid a regular salary. The forger can appear to be a consultant, a computer programmer, or even an author of books that nobody reads. If the forger doesn't appear to make a great deal of money and doesn't play the mystery man, he will blend into middle America fine. The forger makes all of his major "toy" purchases in other regions, and the locals don't see his spending habits. It takes as much concern and determination for the forger to live with the money he steals as it does to steal it. The single most common thing that all criminals share in their work is too much time on their hands. That, along with too much money, are the two things that the average Joe and his family lack. If the forger stands out, the *"have nots"* will bring him down. Their jealousies are the forger's biggest enemies, so he must always be aware of their attention when he does flamboyant things that they cannot or will not do. Those who share the forger's secrets with him will want to get involved, and if he denies them their involvement, they will resent him. Every person will give the forger up if properly motivated, and he is a fool if he thinks otherwise.

Chapter Twenty
An Unethical
Real Estate Scam

There are countless books on making money in the real estate business. I wrote one myself. But the following method is not discussed in any publication I have ever seen or heard about. If it is ever discussed in casual conversation, it is usually in the negative aspect. What I will describe is simple in actuality, as close to illegal as one can get, and as unethical as it is profitable. A Realtor with scruples will most likely not even know what is being discussed here, but since most Realtors are crooks, they will know about it, but will just act as if they don't. It does violate enough civil and ethical rules to guarantee the perpetrator's losing any court action that might come his way as a result of his use of this method, so that makes it close enough to being a crime to qualify it for inclusion in this book. The person that the forger does this to will swear that it is a crime, and you can hardly blame him for thinking so. It is by no means a get-rich-quick scam, but it is a viable way to make a healthy score, and the forger gets to do it while wearing a suit.

The process is actually quite simple. The object is to buy property that the seller is willing to carry a second mortgage on, then foreclose oneself out and buy the property out of foreclosure from the mortgage company. This process eliminates any second or third mortgages which are against the property. If the forger is ready with the necessary financing at the moment of the dissolution of the first mortgage, he can collect the equity that is created by the elimination of any other debts against the property.

Now, once again, but this time in plain English. The idea here is for the forger to assume a first mortgage and not make payments on it, while he *does* make payments on the second mortgage he has with the seller. The first mortgage holder will foreclose on the forger for not making payments to him, while the second mortgage holder is not even aware of what is going on. Since the forger will be making payments to the second mortgage holder, he will not be violating his contract with him. The second mortgage holder has no right to do anything about the forger's other deal, but his awareness of the facts is an irritant the forger should avoid if possible.

The first mortgage holder will begin the process of foreclosure by sending the forger notices and calling him after a couple of months of the forger's ignoring them. The first mortgage holder's job is to try and get the payments from the forger, but he is also trying to protect his company's money. He will make attempts to work something out with the forger, and is not considered an enemy. The forger's job is to do and say whatever is required to force the first mortgage holder to foreclose as soon as possible. This is where this transaction becomes unethical, because the forger has to lie about his intentions to anyone who becomes aware of what's going on. The forger informs those who become concerned that he knows what he is doing, and that his business is not a subject he wishes to discuss. The forger can give the impression that he is planning to refinance in time to solve all his problems, and in the time frame they have indicated. After all, if the forger does not come through in time, the first mortgage holder will have the property, and the forger will lose it. It's a business deal, nothing more. Foreclosures happen all of the time in this business, and it's no big deal to those involved, so the forger acts appropriately.

If the second mortgage holder gets into the picture, the forger will have to convince him that he knows what he is doing and that there is nothing to worry about. If the forger is making his payments to the second mortgage holder, he will assume that the forger must have a plan or something going on that is not readily apparent, or the forger would not be wasting his money on the payments. The argument is logical and easily believed. The process consists of the forger lying his ass off until it's too late for anybody to do anything about it, and then showing up at the foreclosure sale and informing the participating parties that he has made arrangements to buy the entire first mortgage as soon as the clock runs out on the first mortgage contract. The mortgage company's job is to protect their investors' money and to collect all of the outstanding debts in any manner that is legally possible. They are under no obligation to inform any of the other mortgage holders of what is going on. As a matter of fact, the forger should inform the first mortgage holder that the dealings with the other mortgage holders are his business, and any interference in his business practices would not be appreciated and might result in legal action if they were to take unauthorized action in any form other than what is expressed in the contract. This is a strong-arm tactic, but it is legal and happens all of the time.

The first mortgage holder may realize what the forger is doing, but will likely opt for the legally protected methods of covering his ass. He will collect his money, pay his investors, and move on to other things that are not related to the forger's business. It's a dog-eat-dog world, and the mortgage holder broke no laws in his dealings, so all that can happen is that the forger can be sued in civil court, and the mortgage holder he was dealing with will probably recommend that the others sue the forger, but it will be after the fact, and only done to look as if he were really concerned. Since the forger will be in a position to have the property frozen by a court action, the mortgage holder will sell it as soon as possible. The forger takes his profit and walks away, letting the buyer and the others fight over the property. This might sound like a lot of trouble, but the potential for a large score is there if the forger cares to do his homework.

Chapter Twenty One
To Recap

The prospect of getting a computer, setting it up with the various other pieces of equipment, and making it work properly may sound overwhelming. The prudent forger will take the time to go over the steps enough times to familiarize himself with the process and reduce the anxiety. To most people who are not familiar with computers, they seem cold and foreign-appearing. Many people overcome those very feelings when they receive adequate instruction. The most important factor is the forger's desire and willingness to try. Without that effort, there is little that can be done to motivate him. Tuning up one's car requires greater skill and is more difficult than using computers to make or alter documents. The term *"user-friendly"* refers to how easily the computer does the things the user wants done on it. Today's computers are very user-friendly. If the forger can hunt and peck on a typewriter and follow simple directions such as: *"Move the cursor to the part of the document you want to change"* and press *"Enter,"* then he is easily able to use and succeed on most computers. When the forger purchases software for his computer, he tells the salesman that he needs a model that comes with good instructions and a built-in "Help" function. The salesman will direct the forger to the products that he wants. There are different versions of most programs, so the forger must make sure that he gets the features he wants in them. Most advanced programs assume that the user has the knowledge to use them and doesn't need additional instructions. Since cost is always an issue, they include only what *they* think the user will need, not what *the user* thinks he will need. If the forger uses a salesman when he shops for software, things will go much smoother.

The actual hands-on usage is so easy that once the forger does it, he immediately realizes how foolish his fears of incompetence were. I have been using computers and teaching their use since they were first introduced to the general public in the mid-seventies, and all I can say is that computers are a piece of cake compared to programming a damned VCR. Every day computers become more user-friendly. I am now using one that follows voice commands. Both of my sons are rocket scientists compared to me. If the fledgling forger were to devote the same time and energy to studying computers as he would to learning how to run the cash register at a 7-Eleven job, he would be a pro in no time. Remember, even a Ferrari starts at zero. If the forger plays his cards right, he can buy one and see for himself.

When the forger sets out to do some of the crimes discussed in this book, the preparations he makes before and during the crime will be the difference between doing it and doing it *right*. If the forger has set up the proper IDs and has made correct arrangements to cash the checks and erase all traces of his presence, he is starting to get the *big* picture. There are two ways to do anything in life: the right way... and all of the other ways.

It doesn't matter which versions of crime the forger is doing; the check-cashing is the one factor that always makes the difference in the actual amount of net profit he realizes, versus what he *could* have taken in. If the forger takes the time to travel to the places he intends to do a crime in, and opens up the bank accounts at least 30 days prior to his crime, he will increase his percentage of success by a factor that will make a big difference in the long run. I have done it both ways, and it seems that it doesn't matter most of the time, but the times it mattered, it *really* mattered. The further in advance the accounts are opened the better. The forger will learn how to deal with bank cashiers and loan officers quickly. Soon the forger will see that they are no different than any other fish in the sea. If the forger has the gift of gab (and in this business it is a major plus) this profession is his calling. Fraud crime is actually quite fun, if the forger lets it become so. DMVs are for getting IDs and licenses, and banks are for banking and cashing checks: it's what they are there for. Nothing the forger will be doing is out of the ordinary, and if he acts normally, he will not alert anyone who might otherwise remember him. Dressing for the part and acting like a normal person are part of the game the forger is playing. His appearance and manners are props in a play. If the forger **never** forgets that the critics carry badges, he might not win an Oscar, but at least he can afford to buy one if he wants to.

Other Points That the Forger Always Remembers Are:

1. When the forger is opening accounts or cashing checks, savings and loan institutions are just as good as regular banks; they just have fewer branches.

2. If one DMV outlet says no, it doesn't tell the others about the forger's attempt.

3. If one DMV outlet issues the forger an ID, it doesn't tell the others it did so.

4. The forger could get a different ID from each DMV outlet in the city.

5. The forger should avoid getting IDs from states that mail them, as his photo is kept on file and he needs a real address to receive the ID.

6. If applying for a passport, the forger always uses someone else's fingerprints on the mail-in application.

7. The forger is always aware of his fingerprints, and who is taking and keeping a photograph of him for any reason. This includes girlfriends, too.

8. The forger is always aware of where he parks his car, and who sees him in it.

9. The forger avoids personal relationships in cities where he does crime. It's business.
10. Check protectors are more than worth the effort.
11. Bonded credit cards are easy to get and are a must in most fraud crimes.
12. The forger uses his ATM card to check on his account before he goes into banks.
13. Taking a weapon into any bank constitutes armed robbery, regardless of the person's intentions, or whether or not the weapon is concealed.
14. Magnetic ink is always used on the checks the forger prints.
15. It is foolish for the forger to carry more than one set of ID on his person at one time.
16. It is best for the forger to avoid traveling by airplane if possible, as air travelers are heavily scrutinized.
17. If the forger must fly, he buys his tickets at an agency. He keeps in mind that check-ins are filmed for security reasons, and luggage is x-rayed.
18. If arrested, the forger has approximately 48 hours to make bail and split. False ID is not suspected unless there is some reason, and is seldom discovered through a standard arrest. Most times, the authorities never discover it, and if the forger is not armed, bail is usually low.
19. It is best to remember the previous eighteen points.

Chapter Twenty Two
The Last Word (So Far)

I would like to throw in a word to the wise concerning crimes of fraud. It is like any other big business, inasmuch as the money which has been stolen or diverted has to go through a bank of some kind somewhere along the line. And most banks don't really have hundreds of thousands of dollars just lying around waiting for us to come in and free it. So, if the forger perpetrates a crime that involves the removal of actual cash from a bank, he runs into the same problem that a bank robber does: the cash is just not there. The forger can run all over town and get a little cash from each branch, but it doesn't really amount to the total that he could get if the cash were available all in one place. The forger cannot go into a bank in this country and expect to walk out with any large amount of cash ("large" being defined as anything over ten thousand dollars). The system is designed to give a little to a lot, and when one attempts to get a lot, the machine goes into overdrive to prevent or deter it from happening. If a customer asks a teller for an amount of cash over her limit (usually a grand), she must call the manager for an override approval and signature. The manager appears, and the customer's request is then scrutinized with the vigor of the Gestapo. It goes beyond protecting their interest; it borders on being insulting. If I weren't there to steal, I would never do business in an *Amerikan* bank. They are rude and arrogant, and I love to beat them.

This is the major drawback to big-ticket crimes of fraud, and it's the stopper in all types of crimes that depend upon getting large amounts of cash out of a bank. Since the only dependable way to remove cash is in small increments, most scams run out of time with only a few hundred grand as the prize. I have seen many fraud crimes, mine included, that put a million dollars or more in the bank, yet only a portion of that amount was realized in the end. That is why the forger needs to concentrate on crimes that have a ceiling of a couple of hundred grand and the methods needed to get that sum *out* of the banks. That is why good fraud crimes take such dedicated preparation.

The forger often opens up several bank accounts and a business (or two) in the city he plans on hitting. By doing so, he opens up more avenues to get cash from, and thus increases his chances of netting more. Since it really involves actually walking into a bank to get the cash, it quickly becomes obvious that the forger is physically limited in just how many places he can get to in a business day. The ideal situation for the efficient forger is to plan his route well in advance and keep to his schedule. The forger can hire people to do this for him, and that increases the take. But is it worth it for all of those people to know the forger's business and his face? These are not problems which are encountered by the petty criminal, but neither are the amounts of money under discussion. If the forger is not up to addressing the complexities of this profession, the sooner he realizes it the better off he will be. Current *white collar* penalties are severe, and they are getting worse every day. The public is starting to wake up to the amounts of money being lost in this sector, and the laws are being adjusted accordingly. If the forger acts like a smart criminal, he is considered in a different category than a bank robber or armed robber. In most cases, they will get less time than a big-time forger, because the public fears them less. Acts of violence are generally poorly planned or spontaneous, and that's what the system is set up to deal with. *Brain crime* bothers the money institutions, and they are the real heavy hitters in the law business. They want the forger and his ideas off the streets and out of their banks. The forger will most likely get a break the first time he's caught, if the amount is not too large, but if he gets caught again a pattern starts to emerge. The terms *continuing criminal enterprise* and *career criminal* will be applied to the forger, or, indeed, to any form of crime that has employees or requires brains to commit. Once the forger has these phrases attached to his record, he is marked for life. Most of the escapades I have mentioned in this book would be considered "brain crimes," and the rules are very different than one might think. I am not saying that it is not worth it. As far as I am concerned, there is no other way to live than the way one wants to. If that way is by doing crime to finance one's lifestyle, then the criminal should at least do the crimes that pay well, and keep violence to a minimum. If one can go to jail for driving without a license, or not having insurance, or not paying alimony, then I think there is something more than just a little wrong with this country's laws. At least my lifestyle justifies the risk.

I believe that family and friends are important: I have both. I also believe that if a person cannot live the way he wants to, he might as well be in prison. I do not know what prison is to others, but to me it is a place to reflect and dream of tomorrow. The one thing that a person in jail has over his jailers is something very hard to explain to someone who has not gone through it. When the doors are opened and he is released, he experiences a feeling that borders on being born again. It's a new start or beginning; the air is new, life feels great, the touch of a woman is like the first time revisited. This is a state of mind that cannot easily be explained, but can only be felt. Ask a freed prisoner of war, or a soldier who has been long absent; they know the feeling, and *that* feeling is part of the game. I have made my bed and I sleep very well in it. I look forward to things that the average person has grown bored with. I have a light in my eyes that others comment on. I see it in very few others... and I have never seen it in the eyes of a sheep.

It's All Worth It, Including the Final Crash...

Back in the game!

An Insider's Guide
to Unwritten Rules
Compiled by Jesse M. Greenwald

Remember: If you haven't spotted the mark in the first half hour at the table, it's you.

1. A thousand friends are not enough, but a single enemy often is.

2. No man's credit is worth as much as his cash.

3. Believe the *man* – not the oath.

4. If you are the anvil, be patient. If you are the hammer, *strike!*

5. Nothing weighs less than a promise.

6. If you are forced to bow, bow very, very low, and hold that bitter memory until you can take revenge.

7. The wife of a careless man is almost a widow.

8. To make a point, try something sharp!

9. Wolves may lose their teeth, but never their nature.

10. Silence makes few mistakes.

142

11. The wrong choice usually seems the more reasonable.

12. Never make an enemy whom you don't have to.

13. Women, wind, and luck change often.

14. All who snore are not sleeping.

15. Money is always welcome, even if it comes in a dirty sack.

16. Opportunity makes the thief. The thief who has no opportunity to steal calls himself an honest man.

17. A mask has two sides.

18. Occasionally suffer fools, as you may learn something useful. But never argue with one!

19. You cannot put a good edge on bad steel.

20. Victories are always temporary, as are defeats. Learn from both.

21. Perseverance is the key that so few ever turn.

22. Fortune smiles... then betrays!

23. A handful of luck is worth more than a truckload of wisdom.

24. If you cannot win, then make the price of your enemy's victory so exorbitant he never forgets.

25. Open your wallet and your mouth cautiously.

26. Always draw the snake from the hole with another man's hand.

27. Money scammed is twice as sweet as money earned, and often more so.

28. If you allow your friends or your enemies to think they are your equals, they will immediately assume they are your superiors.

29. When skating on thin ice, skate fast!

30. When you are angry, close your mouth and open your eyes.

31. Strike first, and you will strike last.

32. What goes around, comes around... but just not soon enough for most people.

33. Money may not be able to buy happiness, but it provides the time to search for it.

34. A strategically placed mirror allows for the occasional turn of the back.

35. When letting "sleeping dogs" lie, ensure that they are in fact sleeping.

36. Tempting those whom you know cannot resist temptation proves nothing you didn't already know, except to those whom you may not have wished to know it.

37. A man who will not accept your money is accepting someone else's.

38. Pay for what you get, and get what you pay for.

39. Enemies with a common cause are still enemies.

40. Partners provide many things, including testimony.

41. No matter how short the skirt, there's always room for a wire.

42. Promises, like wine, will turn to vinegar if handled poorly.

43. An unloaded gun makes a poor club.

44. Love is stronger than Kevlar, but as fragile as china.

45. When driving down a mountain, check your own brakes.

144

46. A friend in need is a friend indeed.

47. Six feet is never deep enough, if more than one dig the hole.

Note: Rules are only effective if you use them, even if it hurts. If they weren't difficult to live by, you wouldn't need them, now would you? If you think they are unfair or that you might know better, don't lose any sleep over it. Those who will use them when dealing with you won't.

Jesse M. Greenwald

YOU WILL ALSO WANT TO READ:

YOU WILL ALSO WANT TO READ (Continued)

☐ **40050 MAKING CRIME PAY,** *by Harold S. Long.* What does it take to succeed at a criminal activity? What does it take to make crime pay? Written by a professional criminal, this book delves deeply into the realities of the criminal justice system and offers many hard-won suggestions for successfully evading the system. It is packed with information not available anywhere else (except, maybe, in jail). It explains what makes some criminals successful while others get caught. It also discusses how to deal with police, courts, and the criminal justice system to minimize apprehension and conviction. Everything you read here will be fact recounted in part from personal experiences, and in part from the experiences of inmates across the country. *1988, 5½ x 8½, 81 pp, soft cover.* $9.95.

☐ **91085 SECRETS OF A SUPER HACKER,** *by The Knightmare, with an Introduction by Gareth Branwyn.* The most amazing book on computer hacking ever written! Step-by-step, illustrated details on the techniques used by hackers to get at your data including: Guessing Passwords; Stealing Passwords; Password Lists; Social Engineering; Crashing Electronic Bulletin Boards; Dummy Screens; Fake e-mail; Trojan Horses; Viruses; Worms; How to keep from getting caught; And much more! The how-to text is highlighted with bare-knuckle tales of the Knightmare's hacks. No person concerned with computer security should miss this amazing manual of mayhem. *1994, 8½ x 11, 205 pp, illustrated, soft cover.* $19.95.

Loompanics Unlimited
PO Box 1197
Port Townsend, WA 98368

DFCD7

Please send me the books I have checked above. I have enclosed $_____ which includes $4.95 for shipping and handling of the first $20.00 ordered. Add an additional $1 shipping for each additional $20 ordered. Washington residents include 7.9% sales tax.

Name _____

Address _____

City/State/Zip_____

VISA and MasterCard accepted. 1-800-380-2230 for credit card orders *only.*
8am to 4pm, PST, Monday through Friday.

YOU WILL ALSO WANT TO READ (Continued)

☐ **10065 HOW TO HIDE THINGS IN PUBLIC PLACES,** *by Dennis Fiery.* Did you ever want to hide something from prying eyes, yet were afraid to do so in your home? Now you can secrete your valuables away from home, by following the eye-opening instructions contained in this book, which identifies many of the public cubbyholes and niches that can be safely employed for this purpose. Absolutely the finest book ever written on the techniques involved in hiding your possessions in public hiding spots, profusely illustrated with over 85 photographs. Also contains an appendix of Simplex lock combinations. *1996, 5½ x 8½, 220 pp, illustrated, soft cover.* $15.00.

☐ **10066 HOW TO USE MAIL DROPS FOR PROFIT, PRIVACY AND SELF-PROTECTION,** *by Jack Luger.* There are many reasons you might want to use a mail drop: nomads use no fixed address; if your mail has been stolen from your residential mailbox; to keep creditors and correspondents at arm's length; to keep your actual whereabouts secret, and much more. Mail drops are the number one most important technique for insuring your privacy. They are confidential mailing addresses that allow you to receive and send mail anonymously. How to select a mail drop; Private safe deposit boxes; Sex in the mail; Law enforcement and mail drops; Financial privacy; Electronic mail drops; And much more. Several lists by state and city. *1996, 5½ x 8½, 184 pp, soft cover.* $16.95.

Loompanics Unlimited
PO Box 1197
Port Townsend, WA 98368

DFCD7

Please send me the books I have checked above. I have enclosed $_____ which includes $4.95 for shipping and handling of the first $20.00 ordered. Add an additional $1 shipping for each additional $20 ordered. Washington residents include 7.9% sales tax.

Name _____

Address _____

City/State/Zip _____

VISA and MasterCard accepted. 1-800-380-2230 for credit card orders *only*.
8am to 4pm, PST, Monday through Friday.